Due Dec 10

WITHDRAWN

Japan Quality Control Circles

Asian Productivity Organization
TOKYO

Companion volumes in this series
RELIABILITY GUIDEBOOK
PRODUCTION ENGINEERING
MANUAL ON PLANT LAYOUT AND MATERIALS HANDLING
PRODUCTION PLANNING AND CONTROL
GUIDE TO QUALITY CONTROL
GUIDE TO QUALITY CONTROL CASE STUDIES

Other Asian Productivity Organization Publications

Industrial Organization and Management
AGRIBUSINESS MANAGEMENT RESOURCE MATERIALS
VOLUME 1 – INTRODUCTION TO AGRIBUSINESS MANAGEMENT
VOLUME 2 – AGRIBUSINESS – ASIAN CASE STUDIES PART 1
AGRIBUSINESS – ASIAN CASE STUDIES PART 2

Economic and Industrial Development and Productivity
TRANSFER OF TECHNOLOGY AMONG THE DEVELOPING COUNTRIES
PRODUCTIVITY AND ECONOMIC DEVELOPMENT
PREPARING FEASIBILITY STUDIES IN ASIA

Library of Congress Catalog Card Number: 77-186288

Industrial Engineering and Technology

Japan Quality Control Circles

Quality Control Circle Case Studies

Asian Productivity Organization
TOKYO

Designed and Produced by
SERASIA LIMITED
for
ASIAN PRODUCTIVITY ORGANIZATION
4-14, 8-chome, Akasaka,
Minatoku, Tokyo 107, Japan
© Asian Productivity Organization, 1972
ISBN: 92-833-1022-5 (Limpbound)
       92-833-1021-7 (Casebound)

Second Reprint 1982
Designed and Printed in Hong Kong by
NORDICA INTERNATIONAL LIMITED

TS
156
J33

Contents

	Page
Introduction	1
The advancing QC Circle movement	5
The QC Circle and human relationships	15
QC Circle activities and implementation of QC techniques	30
The QC Circle and training	40
Smaller enterprises and QC Circle activities	52

Cases

Case 1
   Eliminating machining errors — 63

Case 2
   Reduction of dimensional defects in felt — 71

Case 3
   Rewind cutting process improved — 81

Case 4
   Reduction of defects in metal plates — 87

Case 5
   Reducing refrigerator component processing defects — 95

Case 6
   Simplification of the weighing of rubber compounding ingredients — 103

Case 7
   Replacement of intermediate inspection by independent inspection — 109

Case 8
   Reduction of raw silk sticking — 117

Case 9
   Reduction of defective soldering work in assembling electrical appliances — 125

	Page
Case 10 Taking the leadership in quality control	133
Case 11 Early operation of newly installed machinery	141
Case 12 Increasing efficiency by improving operation methods	149
Case 13 Improvement of the operating rate of synthetic yarn spinning	159
Case 14 Providing incentives to the QC Circle through an evaluation system	167
Case 15 Reduction in deflection of gear shafts	173
Case 16 Improvement in cylinder bore smoothness	179
Case 17 The QC Circle movement (applied to shop requirements	187
Case 18 Elimination of inspection in the 'A' packing process	199

Introduction

It is both an honour and a privilege to have been invited by the Asian Productivity Organization to write the Introduction to this important book. I feel that the original publisher, the Nikkan Kogyo Shimbun, and the Asian Productivity Organization deserve both our congratulations and our thanks for having made available to the world this remarkably frank and honest account of the Quality Control Circle movement.

"What is the secret of Japan's astonishing industrial growth?" This question prefaces innumerable discussions in the business and technical journals of the western world. Many reasons have been adduced, but in the main these have been based on brief visits, which have allowed observers insufficient opportunity to study Japanese industry in breadth and depth.

Now, thanks to this book, we are provided with source material which makes a valuable contribution to our understanding of this phenomenon of recent times.

It is important to state at once that this is a book for senior managers. They would be missing something of real value were, they to construe its title as denoting a work concerned primarily with a new development of interest only to those directly involved in quality control. Quality Control Circles represent something which is much bigger, much more fundamental to management, than quality control as it is understood in most western countries. The Circles are, basically, an effective means by which the senior managements of a large sector of Japanese industry have succeeded in involving their employees in the aims and the purpose of their enterprises. This involvement, and the special factors which have made the Quality Control Circle movement possible, are underlying reasons for Japan's rapid rate of progress.

Without a proper understanding of these factors it could be all too easy to assume that the movement was equally applicable, in its existing form, in other countries. A study of this book will help the managements of firms in other countries to avoid what might prove to be costly mistakes. At the same time, they will be helped towards a better understanding of the principles of successful management which have been so clearly recognized by Japan's senior executives.

This understanding is facilitated by the numerous case-studies, from which we learn how Quality Control Circles were established in a variety of different firms and industries; what difficulties were experienced, and what successes were achieved. The western reader, however, needs to be aware of certain aspects of Japanese life which, because they are so familiar to the authors of this book, receive little notice.

Informed western opinion is amply supported by the case studies described in this book. Western experts who have studied the situation with understanding recognize the following important factors as being particularly relevant to Japanese industry:

1 The great personal ability of the chief executives of leading Japanese companies. These gifted men combine expert engineering knowledge with astute business acumen.
2 The high literacy of Japanese employees. About 80 per cent of shop-floor workers stay at high school until they are 19. During their last three or four years at school they will have had a thorough grounding in mathematics and science. As a consequence, they are able to think statistically and logically. They share the national craving for further education, and this is satisfied by the many training sessions which are presented in-plant and by professional institutions, on radio and on television.
3 The traditional respect for those in authority, which must give to Japanese executives an advantage enjoyed in few other countries today. It is illustrated in this book by the way in which members of Quality Control Circles submit to the monitoring of their attendance at meetings of their Circles.
4 The clear recognition by top management of the important role of the foreman as the ultimate and vital link between executive management and the operative.
5 The widespread understanding of the purpose and principles of quality control, in its Japanese interpretation as a manage-

INTRODUCTION

ment-oriented, overall approach, which has been achieved by two decades of intensive promotion, education and study.

There may be additional factors. Professor Kaoru Ishikawa, for instance, has been quoted as saying that the Quality Control Circle movement is peculiarly Japanese, and difficult to copy by western firms. Be that as it may, it is believed that the five factors listed above indicate major points of difference between Japanese and western industry in general.

It may, therefore, be instructive to look for a moment at the situations which exist in most other countries, both 'developed' and 'developing'. We find that the majority of firms in these countries are headed by financial rather than by technical executives. Shop-floor workers will have little appreciation of statistics. In developed countries they, and their trade unions, often have deep-rooted self-protective attitudes which make it difficult for them to identify themselves with their firm. In India, the employees of one small engineering company can neither read nor write. Yet this firm has an extremely high reputation both for the quality of its products and for its efficient quality performance. This has been achieved by a small executive team which combines sound financial and technical knowledge. Good planning and training have overcome the drawbacks of illiteracy.

In developed countries, on the other hand, there has been a rapidly-diminishing appreciation of the role of the foreman as a manager. This has come about partly through lack of understanding by senior management, and partly through confusion concerning the role of the shop steward. In most countries other than Japan, quality control is still regarded primarily as inspection-based, rather than as an essential constituent of the total management system.

Despite these disadvantages, there are counter-balancing factors which, for the present at any rate, help to diminish the superiority of Japan in the application of Quality Control. Production engineers and quality engineers in western countries might find it difficult to understand why it has been thought necessary in Japan to enlist the assistance of all employees, to solve problems which are not their specific responsibility. These western engineers might be surprised, too, by the dependence upon the lengthy process of problem-solving which is based upon the logic of the cause-effect diagram. The intuitive approach of these engineers, which derives from a pragmatically-based technical education,

3

coupled with long experience, usually enables them to recognize troubles, to diagnose them, and to cure them, extremely quickly.

This, of course, ignores the great value of the Quality Control Circle scheme as a means of motivating workers, and of involving them in the affairs of a company which is young, or rapidly-expanding. When the supply of industrial engineers in Japan has overtaken the rapid growth in demand, Japan's industry will still enjoy the other benefits which have been described.

It therefore behoves the managements of other countries to take a careful look at the advantages already possessed by Japanese firms, and to initiate action to eliminate the weaknesses existing in their own organizations. The important lesson, for western executives in particular, is the great value of leadership, and the benefit to morale and industrial peace of involvement of the workers in the total enterprise.

Quality Control Circles have clearly been appropriate to the situation in Japan. Other methods have been tried in other countries, but with more limited success. In the United States, for example, Zero Defects Campaigns have had some success in certain industries. In Britain, it has been found effective to help the employee to understand the contribution which he makes to the success of the firm which employs him. Some companies achieved notable results by this means, during National Quality and Reliability Year.

Managements, everywhere, and in every industry, must always consider all the factors involved in their particular circumstances, before taking action. With this single proviso, there can be nothing but benefit in making a careful study of the stimulating examples which have been made so generously available in this valuable book.

F. NIXON.

The advancing QC Circle movement

Yasuo Sugimoto*

What are QC Circles?

The QC Circle movement is permeating the fabric of Japanese industry with astonishing rapidity. And it is effective! In fact, America's Dr J. M. Juran, internationally recognized as an authority on quality control, has commented: "The QC Circle movement is a tremendous one which no other country seems able to imitate. Through the development of this movement, Japan will be swept to world leadership in quality." Inquiries about these circles have come in not only from the United States, but also from Western Europe and the Communist bloc.

But in order to understand how this movement has grown, it is first necessary to analyze the QC Circle.

1 The beginning: publication of QC *for the Foreman*

Foremen, and their subordinates as well, now make it a rule to get outside of the company to exchange opinions through QC meetings, QC Circle conferences, and exchange-of-experience seminars. Just 10 years ago, however, factory workers could not even find an opportunity to air their opinions in their own place of work; all production decisions were dictated from above.

One of the most influential organs in the promotion of quality control in Japan is the magazine *Statistical Quality Control*, published by the Union of Japanese Scientists and Engineers (JUSE). The editors of this magazine, having decided that to achieve effective quality control, interest must be aroused in the factory, published, in 1961, a symposium discussion, 'Problems Facing the Shop Foreman.' The writer, then a member of the editorial board, participated in this symposium. And the parti-

---

* Mr Sugimoto is Production Department Manager, Tokyo Shibaura Electric Co., Tokyo.

cipating shop foremen, from several companies, strongly agreed on two points in particular: (1) that there was a need for a QC magazine less remote from the workshop, and (2) that there was a lack of opportunities for foremen to air their opinions outside of the factory, and that this lack was seriously undermining their morale and enthusiasm.

The editorial board responded immediately by setting up a discussion group on 'Duties of the Shop Foreman in Quality Maintenance' at the 11th annual QC conference, held in November, 1961. Shop foremen were invited to join the panel and make their opinions known.

The board further made haste to plan a sister publication *QC for the Foreman* which made its appearance in July, 1962, including in the first issue a summary of the above-mentioned discussion.

On the occasion of its first issue, *QC for the Foreman* invited discussion on how it could best serve in implementing quality control on the factory level. The following policy lines emerged:

1 To place primary emphasis on the dissemination of techniques to increase the capability and improve the level of control exercised by those on the first-line supervisory level through education, training and popularization of techniques.
2 Set the price at a level that would make the magazine accessible to the maximum number of lower-echelon foremen and ordinary workers who would have to buy it with their own money.
3 To organize QC Circles of operators, led by their foremen, which could become the nuclei of quality control activities in the factories.

Thus, the QC Circle was born in Japan. By June, 1962, three circles were registered with the JUSE. By September there were 13 circles with 130 members and by December there were 20, with a membership of 400.

Subsequent growth was amazingly rapid, and now these circles, born in Japan and flourishing in her unique soil, have achieved results which have attracted the interest of the world.

As of September, 1968, there were 16,000 registered QC Circles with a membership of 200,000, and it is a safe estimate that many more circles are not registered.* Surprising is hardly the word!

---

* As of August, 1969, there were 24,000 and JUSE reported the number was increasing by 700 to 1,000 each month.

It is evident that this expansion was only in answer to perception of a correspondingly acute need.

2 Circle objectives

It is obvious that the objectives of the QC Circles will vary considerably from company to company, and according to scale, type of business, and degree of thoroughness of quality control. However some basic generalizations may be made. We may identify the following as QC Circle objectives:

1 To encourage first-line supervisory personnel to educate themselves, and so develop leadership and supervisory capabilities.
2 By including all workers, to raise the morale of the work place, to carry quality control to the ultimate degree, and encourage and develop employees' self-awareness of what quality is, what problems may arise, and what to do about them.
3 To serve as a means of unifying company-wide QC activities and as a nucleus within the shop, and work toward the clarification of executive and managerial policy, stabilization of work-place supervision and guaranteeing of standards.

Introduction of QC Circles to the plant   *Refer to textbook notes*

In any company, there is considerable initial confusion about how to proceed in setting up QC Circles. Actually, the procedure involved varies with different industries, and this is as it should be. The following outline is, therefore, no more than a general guide.

1 First, the significance of the QC Circle movement must be fully understood by top management, executives and personnel, and persons involved in labour relations. Though the QC Circle is a 'first-line' activity, it is obvious that the factory does not exist in a vacuum. It belongs to the larger corporate structure and acts on orders from above. Thus, without the recognition and understanding of those having authority, any programme will be hampered.
2 In plants or companies which lack QC Circle experience, conferences and exchange-of-experience seminars should be organized with the participation of top management, executives, and several of the more aware shop foremen. The presence of several foremen is essential here, as only one man is all to likely to be overawed.

These meetings provide a chance to vividly demonstrate the level of activity of the foremen of competitors, and this stimulus can be turned into the nucleus of QC Circles in the shop.

QUALITY CONTROL CIRCLE CASE STUDIES

There have been cases where QC Circles were started by command from above, but the use of the spoken or printed word alone is not immediately effective, and there is a tendency for workers to regard the whole thing with suspicion. The use of published results attained by other companies, particularly those in the same field, produces especially strong reactions. Actions speak louder than words, and quite naturally produce a desire not to be left behind.

3 QC Circles may then be organized in factories where management is receptive and foremen are aware. It may be a good idea initially to organize a pilot circle composed of foremen only. When it has won a degree of acceptance, circles can be organized around each foreman.

4 Use may also be made of *QC for the Foreman* and other factory-directed publications such as manuals to encourage workers to discuss what measures can be taken in their factory.

5 Three to six months are required for the foremen to assume effective leadership and for all the workers who form the general membership of the circle to be able to speak their minds without reserve.

It is important during this period that management and executives concerned with QC afford cooperation but they must take care not to monopolize discussions. The chairman must always keep in mind that his function is to lead the circle, encouraging the members to free and spontaneous activity. He must try to acquire the habit of not announcing opinions himself but of getting all members to express their opinions.

When all the members can freely express themselves, your QC Circle is in orbit!

6 Once a circle has solved one problem, standardized its operations and stabilized its supervision, it should be led to find and solve other problems, one by one.

Let us next look at some data on the introduction and structure of QC Circles. The data has been derived from answers to questionnaires distributed to circles throughout Japan between November, 1966, and February, 1967.

Initial impetus (total number of persons responding, 530):
    Management directive   44.9%
    Suggestion of executives   33.4%
    Spontaneously   20.9%

Miscellaneous	1.0%	
Membership (total number of persons responding, 429):		
a. All employees	67.8%	(291)
30 persons or more	5.0%	
20-30 persons	11.4%	
10-20 persons	27.4%	
10 persons or less	56.2%	
b. Only some of shop employees:	24.7%	(106)
20 or more persons	1.9%	
10-20 persons	13.1%	
10 persons or less	85.0%	
c. Combined with personnel of other factories:	7.5%	(32)
20 or more persons	12.0%	
10-20 persons	22.5%	
10 or less persons	65.5%	

Circles with a membership of 10 persons or less are thus in an overwhelming majority, a situation which is very convenient in connection with day-to-day direction.

QC Circle direction

Whether a circle, once functioning, can avoid the pitfalls of disintegration on the one hand and hardening into routine formality with consequent loss of effectiveness on the other depends on how well it is directed.

From this point of view, it may be said that the direction of the circle is the most important point, and the one that gives the most trouble.

The course of this direction too necessarily differs according to local company or factory conditions, but an eight-point basic course of action may be outlined here.

1 The circle must not be active only when a problem has been identified. It must remain in existance and active at all times.

Since the QC Circle consists of workers organized around their foreman it involves sharing work experiences and fulfilling daily work norms. Assuming that each day is to show improvement over the one before, certain problems must be solved. The permanence and continuance of the QC Circle is, thus, essential.

On this point, QC Circles are quite different in function from the so-called 'QC project teams' where personnel from different departments form an *ad hoc* group which disbands after solving a specific problem.

2 Emphasis should be placed on autonomous action, with participation of all the members in discussions of control problems and in the implementation of improvements.

If the work is carried out solely in response to direction from above, no feeling of participation will be engendered and a formalistic attitude will develop in which merely following orders is felt to be enough. That worker motivation is given as one objective of QC Circles is due to the need for autonomous direction.

It is said that American factory personnel are hard workers, and that they perform their assigned duties right up to quitting time. However they are simply following rules and have no desire to effect improvement. It is nothing more than a routine 'bookkeeping' attitude toward work. It would certainly be desirable if American workers would adopt the Japanese QC Circle, but the temperament of the workers and American customs make this possibility seem distant.

It is here that Japanese workers shine. Management by participation of all the employees of a company will increase the motivation of all, and the channeling of everyone's knowledge and experience can only bring impressive results.

3 Proposals on production, rationalization, redressing of grievances, and substandard work are now put into actual operation. Once general objectives are determined, the actual procedures for improvement should be worked out in detail in the QC Circle and the results recorded for the company's use.

In this connection, QC examination seminars should be held, in the shops, preferably once a week and at least once a month, to encourage circle activity.

Determining what action the circle should take will be the first problem. It is advisable initially not to get involved in too big a problem, but to concentrate on problems whose remedies lie within the factory itself.

The members can get the feel of solving problems and of carrying out improvements, giving them confidence to go on to tackle bigger questions. This will result in greater long-run effectiveness. Another point is that the problems taken up need not involve quality control. There are abundant problems concerned with reducing absenteeism, improving working conditions and maintaining a clean and tidy shop, on which the circle can cut its teeth.

Meetings should be held regularly. If they are held only in the face of a specific problem, there is the danger that they cease to be held at all. Differing factory conditions preclude the suggestion of specific intervals; it is best to determine frequency in such a way as to maximize effectiveness in each situation.

4 The head of the circle must provide leadership, while getting the full membership to provide motive power. Members as a whole must find the problems, figure out how to solve them, apply the solution, check, standardize, set up regular procedures and make improvements as problems arise. This is the way to stabilize quality control and make sustained progress.

In QC Circle activities, the *sine qua non* is full participation. If reliance is placed on the opinions and ideas of a select few, activities will come to an early end for lack of general appeal and want of results.

But, it is also true that the foreman must gather the reins of leadership if the members are not to become disorganized. He must lead by encouragement.

Again, it is not necessary that the circle leader be the foreman. There are many examples where effective results were achieved by members assuming the leader's post in turn. However in such cases, the foreman should have sufficient stature that he can guide the younger 'leaders' from the sidelines.

5 The strength of the QC Circles is that they are backed by quality control techniques. To solve factory problems and raise control standards, 'QC mindedness' and techniques must be absorbed and digested to the point where they can be put into immediate practice.

Toward this end, reference material including books and periodicals, manuals, as well as audio-visual materials and short courses of instruction, should be utilized.

6 It is essential to meet and coordinate activities with other circles in the company, and hold intra-firm meetings where experience can be shared. Here, management and executives must be careful not to dampen the enthusiasm of the circle leaders. Even if the presentation is poorly organized, it is important not to criticize, but to suggest ways to improve it.

If discussions involve only the members of the same circle, the format rapidly becomes stereotyped. In meeting with other circles in the company, members will discover many strong points of which they were unaware, and will thus be stimulated. Inter-circle meetings where members get together with other circles doing related jobs, to understand one another's problems, needs and desires, are particularly advantageous.

Holding meetings to allow exchange of experiences within the factory or department, under the chairmanship of the senior manager involved, injects a note of competition and often produces good results. If the top man comments on each presentation, this will particularly encourage the participants.

7   Exchange visits with QC Circles of other firms, for the mutual raising of standards, also produces good results. These exchanges usually take the form of about 10 circle leaders or members from each company looking over each other's plants, comparing practices, and discussing problems.

Since ordinary workers have few chances to see other companies, this can be an educational activity, serving to broaden their horizons. It will often result in their being spurred on by the good points they observe at the other plant. Some companies arrange for exchange visits on their own, but it is more common to do so through the QC Circle Headquarters (located within the JUSE) or its branch office. It has long been felt that such exchanges are effective in raising standards.

8   Once the QC Circle has begun to function it should obtain registration and take part in inter-firm conferences, foremen's QC conferences and the activities of the local QC Circle branch office.

Registration simply means informing the QC Circle headquarters. The only formality is to complete the QC Circle Registration Card, published in *QC for the Foreman* and send it to the headquarters.

QC Circle Conference: QC Circles engage in a number of activities which cross company lines. These include circle conferences (comprising exchanges of experience, panel discussions, intra-departmental discussion groups, QC open meetings, special lectures and plant inspections), exchange visits, inspection trips and lectures. The QC Circle conferences have increased every year. They have become coordinated with operations and have produced such good results that they are among the outstanding facets of Japan's quality control movement.

Since the examples presented at these conferences immediately relate to those who actually do the work, they strike a responsive chord in the participants, and the remedies suggested are in concrete terms and thus directly applicable.

In order to provide maximum opportunity for QC Circle conference participants to give their opinions, procedural decisions should be left to the foremen, and the chairman should be chosen at random from among the participants.

From the time the first conference of this kind was held in Sendai City in 1963, to February, 1968, 52 have been held. There were, in those conferences, 28,848 individual participants, 4,245 corporate participants, and 2,524 presentations.

The Conference of Medium and Small Business QC Circles, which was held in Tokyo in October, 1968, was No. 76, and now not a month goes by without a QC Circle conference being held somewhere in Japan.

QC Circle Headquarters and its Branches: The Headquarters of the QC Circle movement is part of the JUSE, and in order for organization of circles to keep pace with the growth of the movement, five branches have been established for the Kanto, Tokai, Hokuriku, Kinki, Chugoku and Shikoku regions, each headed by an executive from one of the larger companies operating in the region. These branches organize circle activities, and such branch-sponsored events have increased recently.

The above is a picture of circle organization, but in the last analysis the executives and managers concerned with quality control must provide skillful leadership if boredom is not to set in and members decide to give up.

Thus, the intelligent cooperation of executives and management is absolutely essential for the continuation of the circles and the raising of their effectiveness.

There are a great many difficult operational problems such as scheduling of meetings and compensating workers for activities outside of working hours. The following results of a questionnaire distributed to QC-conscious companies may suggest what has been found suitable in Japan.

Scheduling of meetings (total responses: 448)
    Outside working hours   43.5%
    During working hours   31.7%
    Irregular   24.8%
Scheduling when held outside of working hours
(total responses: 393)
    After work   38.2%
    Lunch hour   8.7%
    Morning   3.1%

Provision for compensation for extra time spent
(total responses: 422)
   Provided   71.3%
   Not provided   28.7%
Form of compensation (total responses: 320)
   Normal overtime rate   80%
   Self-improvement bonus   10%
   Meal expenses   1.6%
   Miscellaneous   8.4%
Length of average QC Circle meeting
   Less than 30 minutes   23%
   30 — 60 minutes   42%
   60 — 90 minutes   6%
   90 — 120 minutes   28%
   more than 120 minutes   1%

The QC Circle and human relations

Kozo Koura*

This is hardly the first time that the subject of QC Circles and human relations has been taken up. It is my intention in this article to look at this question from a standpoint of respect of and reliance on the individual, i.e. with some use of western thought on the subject, and on this presumption, to adduce a number of examples to illustrate how circle members, their leaders, managers, and instructors approach the matter.

This question is so complex and multi-faceted that it is virtually impossible to cover it fully. The author therefore requests the reader's understanding if his treatment should appear incomplete.

Exposition of the problem

Whenever we attend a QC Circle conference or a study consultation meeting of the JUSE-sponsored Foremen's Basic Course seminars, the question that always crops up in discussions with the foremen is 'human relations.' For example, they ask

What is one to do about those who turn their backs on the activities of the circle?

How can teamwork be developed?

How can everyone's energies be concentrated on reaching the objective?

These are among the problems that trouble the conscientious circle leader, and we ourselves have no pat answers either.

'So many men, so many minds.' In every man is reflected his environment, and this variety of mental processes brings on many complex problems. Difficult it may be to isolate the thread that untangles the knot.

---

* Mr Koura is Control Manager, Control Bureau, Nippon Kayaku Co., Tokyo, a maker of explosives, dyes and other products.

However we cannot just fold our arms and let things go. We must grapple aggressively with the problem and redouble our efforts.

This is because the operation of any enterprise is grounded on its personnel, and the basis of activity in the factory is human relations.

We take the liberty here of reproducing figure 1 from "Production and Leadership," an article in *QC for the Foreman,* no. 20, written by Kyoji Kirishima and Miss Katsuko Nishigaki of Nippon Rayon Co.'s Uji plant, who were the recipients of the first annual Foreman's QC Prize in 1965.

It suggests that there are four elements which are necessary in improving factory relations:
1   Good supervisors
2   Good workers
3   Supervisor—worker relations
4   A pleasant working place

In considering the QC Circle and human relations, I would like to follow this list of 'essential attributes' and distinguish two aspects:
1   Human relations as a prerequisite for circle activities, and
2   The influence of these activities on such relations

Human relations as a prerequisite for Circle activities

1   The fundamental stream of QC circle activity
I wish all my readers to note the unbroken stream of respect for and reliance on the individual which permeates Dr Juran's interpretation.

Dr Juran in his article, "The QC Circle Phenomenon," which appeared in the January, 1967, issue of the American magazine, *Industrial Quality Control,* says:

"Of the utmost importance is the fact that, through the QC Circles, the Japanese have made a clean break with a tired, outworn theory which plagues the West. This is the theory that the company's quality troubles are due to operator indifference, blunder and even sabotage. Under this theory, the operators could solve the company's quality problems if only the right motivational lever could be found and thrown.

"The QC Circle concept starts with a different set of beliefs:
We don't really know the cause of our quality troubles; we don't even know which are the main troubles. Hence,

THE QC CIRCLE AND HUMAN RELATIONS

Figure 1 Cause-and-effect diagram of human relations

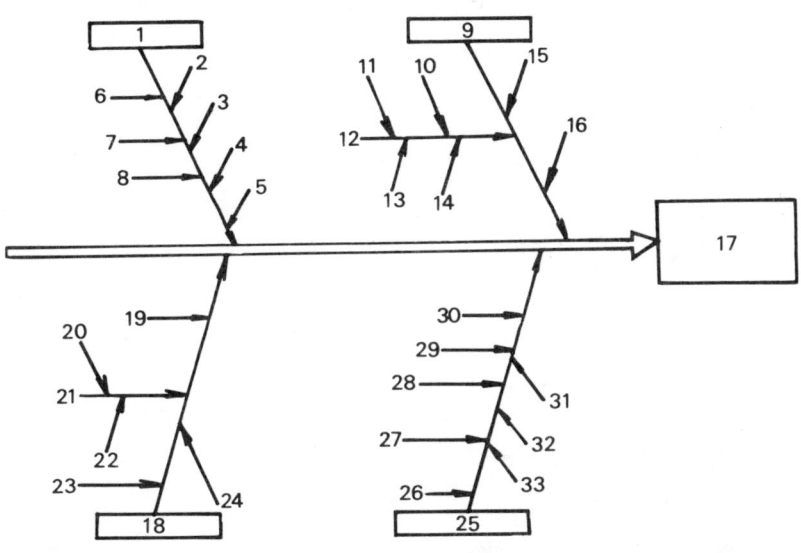

1. Good worker
2. Cooperativeness
3. Sense of responsibility
4. Motivated
5. Healthy
6. Sociability with co-workers
7. Competitiveness in a good sense
8. Does not complain about work
9. Good supervisor
10. Listens to subordinates' suggestions
11. Method of instruction
12. Leadership ability
13. Just and fair
14. Puts himself in subordinates' shoes
15. Devoted to duty
16. Clear-cut policies
17. How to improve human relations
18. Supervisor-worker relations
19. Mutual referral of problems
20. Appreciation of others' intentions
21. Discussion
22. Gives opinions frankly
23. Thinks of others' points of view
24. United effort
25. A pleasant working place
26. Improved atmosphere
27. Improved relations with up-line and down-line workers
28. Teamwork
29. Safe work
30. Absence of injustice and dissatisfaction
31. A feeling that working is worthwhile
32. A place where it is enjoyable to work
33. A place with a good environment

17

we must teach people how to analyze the trouble pattern to identify the main troubles. Also,
we must teach people how to list the suspected causes of the main troubles, and how to discover which are the real causes.

Then
we must help people to secure remedies for these real causes.
Finally,
we must teach people how to hold the gains through modern control methods."

2 The good supervisor

Some qualities necessary in the good supervisor are that he have a clear plan of action, that he be personally diligent, that he be fair, and clear in giving directions, that he constantly put himself in his subordinates' shoes, and that he listen to their expressed opinions. Yasuo Matsuzawa of Toyota Motor Co., Ltd. in an article in *QC for the Foreman*, no. 27, discusses this. Calling on foremen to improve human relationships in order to develop the firm determination required of idealistic new recruits fresh out of school, to allow them to stand up to the competitive world of business, he writes as follows:

1 We employees receive satisfaction from taking responsibility for the completion of our assigned tasks. This satisfaction gives meaning to our lives and provides us with a feeling of pride.

2 Our livelihood is dependent on the company, and we believe that as it prospers, so does our economic position improve, fear of hardship diminish, and we are able to lead a fuller life.

3 When substandard goods are discovered, we strive to find the cause and strive to prevent a recurrence. We therefore appreciate it when our superiors try to understand our position and refrain from making the decisions themselves.

4 In our work, good health is the most important thing. We therefore wish our superiors to be solicitous and considerate in both word and deed.

5 Since we have a strong and heart-felt interest in company actions in relation to the changing currents of society at large, we hope that we will be kept fully and factually informed, not merely by house organs and union newsletters, but by having the opportunity of direct discussion with our superiors.

6 If we have a problem, we want sincere advice, not just a lacing for shortcomings. We want a man who will give opportunity for reflecting on the work and on whom we can depend.

To say the same thing in a different way, the supervisor must recognize the precise role of each basic function, and must have a keen appreciation for problems combined with a well developed ability to solve them. He must have a strong personality backed by vitality. He must treat his subordinates not as cogs in an impersonal organization but as the main figures in the productive process. He must assign work as a meaningful task and through these tasks seek to develop their knowledge, skills and attitude so that they will become at the earliest possible date fully responsible adults able to 'think with their own brain and move on their own feet.' And is it not this kind of organizer who will help them, firmly yet kindly, by look and by deed; who will work actively for his superiors and who can move both subordinates and superiors?

3 A good worker

The attributes of the ideal worker are cooperativeness, sense of responsibility, good health, sociability and a good competitive spirit. He is a person who does not complain about his work, who realizes the importance of his work and who does his best.

Since a QC Circle is a small group, formed by individual workers, its members must study and absorb the idea of quality control, develop an awareness of problems, and move forward with steady determination.

Here are a few of the slogans which, through various channels, are directed at QC Circle members:

Raise the level of human reliability
Become a person with a sales point
Re-examine yourself quality control-wise
Strengthening each individual strengthens the group
Turn your gaze overseas and start a QC Circle
Every day a renewal
Break down the status quo

It is when every member strives in this spirit, continuing autonomous and self-educating activities that the permanence of the QC Circle can be assured.

QUALITY CONTROL CIRCLE CASE STUDIES

4 Relations between supervisors and workers

The most important factor presented here is 'communication' based on trust. It is necessary that all discuss freely what they think, improve mutual understanding, act only after considering everyone's point of view, and build a framework of cooperation in which everyone is united in common endeavour.

This is built on mutual trust, and the attitude of everyone accepting the challenge of a goal set by all the workers together under the leadership of good supervisors is highly desired.

Let us here quote from an article by Nario Ishiguro of Mitsubishi Heavy Industries, Ltd., appearing in *QC for the Foreman*, no. 30.

"I am in charge of the assembly of small marine diesel engines, We have long employed quality control and had virtually solved all our technological problems, but a number of human problems remained. Such cases as failure to report the discovery of mistakes, refusal to listen to the criticism of those further down the line and lack of penitence when a piece of work, having to be done over totalled more than 15 a month.

"I concentrated on personal relations, which were at the root of all these troubles and brought these human problems up before the QC Circle in order to unify the thinking of the subforemen. The result — the circle's response — was as follows.

" 'In order to maintain and raise quality standards, it is necessary to work in a standardized fashion, take immediate measures if mistakes are discovered, and make sure such mistakes are not repeated. To this end, information from the workers is of great assistance, and is indeed the most important factor. Thus the supervisor must weigh carefully his relations with the younger workers and his attitude toward subordinates who are stubborn or who are responsible for rejects. He must take pains to become a man who enjoys the trust of his subordinates, and who creates an atmosphere in which they will automatically keep him informed.'

"I have always tried to control people psychologically in order to improve quality, and I have always believed that if relations between superiors, equals, and subordinates are improved and planning and directives made clear, human relations will remain sound even if a strict line is pursued in regard to quality. I thus formulated the recommendation of the circle into a concrete policy and left its implementation up to my group leader.

This policy was:

1. Maintain firm loyalty to the plan and exhort cooperation.
2. Accept all information and complaints and keep discussions on a friendly basis.
3. Explain the outcome of any unfortunate incidents, and increase the will to cooperate.
4. Develop the habit of spontaneous checking; inquire about the present checking procedures of the workers.
5. Though it is necessary also to praise the man, emphasis should be placed on praising the work.

"The implementation of this policy with an emphasis not on individual responsibility for mistakes, but on a solution arrived at by a conference of all section members was combined with encouragement of active participation in social and athletic activities within the section to loosen tensions. The result was that group cooperation and trustworthiness were heightened and as a result quality and morale improved. This was reflected in the following specifics:

1. More information was forthcoming from the workers and they were more careful among themselves.
2. The former average of over 15 incidents per month was reduced to two or three.
3. The amount of time spent on repeat or repair work was reduced from 50 or 60 hours to about 10.

"If it is constantly pressed upon the workers that they needn't have the whole picture, it is hard for them to become interested, and they may easily go to the opposite extreme. On the other hand they will be actively interested if they study on their own initiative to acquire knowledge. If they know the significance of what they are doing, and its relative importance, they will turn to it with a will."

There is another method: the company's superiors or executives, or outside instructors, may attempt to lead and educate circle members. In this connection, I refer you to the experience of Bridgestone Tire's Sueyasu Hisao, as told in the October, 1968 issue of *Factory Management*. He was in charge of training in a shop where discontent was rife, resignations common, and absenteeism endemic. In his two years at his post, Sueyasu solved these problems, and at the same time reduced rejects and raised efficiency.

5 A pleasant (personally rewarding) factory

A pleasant and rewarding place to work is one with a good environment or atmosphere, good relations with the processes which preceed and follow it, safe working conditions, teamwork, and absence of discontent. If these are the kind of human relations in which QC activities are carried on, they can hardly help but be satisfying.

Here, there are six main factors: human relations, willingness, functioning, training, time, and shop environment; to which are attached numerous subfactors. But human relations are at the root of everything. From this point of view it is obvious that even training, time, and environment which are not directly connected with the first three factors, must rely on human relations for support.

In ascertaining whether a shop or circle has such characteristics or not, self-examination meetings and questionnaires will, in all likelihood, prove extremely effective. For reference, I have appended table 1 which is a typical questionnaire, developed by Hiroshi Kano of Honshu Paper Manufacturing Co. in an article "Toward Even Greater Development of QC Circles" in *QC for the Foreman,* no. 36.

This pleasant shop of ours must, then, in one sense, be one in which it is rewarding to be and work. Thus it must also be a place of diligent application to the job at hand.

Human desire is said to exist on five levels: physiology, security (high wages), society (a feeling of belonging), self-respect, and self-realization (recognition of one's abilities). It is also said that happiness is achieved when these desires are satisfied by one's own efforts. There is thus no doubt that happiness is the satisfaction of the highest of these desires, that for self-realization.

However we must grasp that there are two ways of looking at this self-realization: The desire to obtain recognition can be either on the basis of improving your own ability as a means to such recognition, or of bettering yourself, passing your improved abilities on to and through others, and thus contributing to the shop, company, or society of which you are a part, and thus earning the recognition of those around you.

This kind of personal growth is developed by the confidence which springs from having overcome an obstacle, and it is in the kind of intimate group typified by the QC Circle that this development takes place. The QC Circle must possess this atmosphere of diligence.

Here is an example of a circle which combined this atmosphere of diligence with a pleasant environment. The subject is "Quality of Sheet Metal Finishing and Human Problems," a report presented by Shizuo Fujiwara, a sub-foreman working for Mitsubishi Heavy Industries Co., at the 1964 Foremen's QC Conference.

Of the sheet metal components produced in this shop in 1955 when the production of aircraft was resumed after a postwar interruption, the reject rate exceeded 10%. The implementation of a variety of quality control techniques and concentration on this problem resulted in reduction to 5% by 1962. Of this, the majority were the result of such man-related factors as lack of skills and faulty workmanship.

As a result of a more conscientious attitude on the part of the workers, that is to say concentration on instilling the habit of self-checking of quality, improvement of skill, and worker education, this has been reduced to the present level of 0.3%.

The prerequisites for this policy of day-to-day education are, first and foremost, determination and daily self-examination on the part of supervisors, as follows:

1   Being a 'good sport' is not enough. He must have firm convictions and policies.
2   He must have the courage to point out the shortcomings of his men.
3   He must get out in front and provide vigorous leadership.

There are further requirements vis-a-vis his subordinates.
1   He must not be too lavish in his praise of his men's skill.
2   He must not criticize every minor point, but rather speak strongly on the over-all picture.
3   If a worker should appear to be losing his enthusiasm, he must counteract by assigning harder, not easier, work.
4   If a worker is having trouble with some difficult task, he should let him struggle along until he comes to a complete dead end; then step in with the advice that will solve things. This will result in an appreciation of the difficulty of productive labor, and at the same time develop a sense of responsibility regarding work.
5   An overlong continuation of tension will only result in inattention. Convenient opportunities to allow a breather should not be missed.

It may be the influence of postwar democratic education, but there is a tendency for people today to exhibit less perseverance and backbone in the face of difficulties.

Therefore, though it may seem on the surface to go against the spirit of the times, a thoroughgoing rigor is required as far as work is concerned; otherwise training becomes impossible, and no progress can be made in eliminating achievement differences within the section. After three years of the policy outlined above, the apprehensively awaited deterioration in human relationships did not materialize. On the contrary, even closer and franker relationships developed.

It does indeed seem that this is the type of factory which will be felt to be a pleasant one.

From the point of view of broad participation, furthermore, giving each member responsibility in turn for one of the operational facets (such as clothing, tidiness, shop beautification, standardization, requisitioning, equipment, safety, measurement, etc.) or assigning each person a topic for research or a specific point to check will be found effective.

The QC Circle will continue to progress in that type of small group with an objective generated spontaneously by the desire of all members to participate in planning, and where all challenge this objective to achieve self-improvement.

The results in terms of human relations

In that the QC Circle is a movement which is based on human reliability, there hardly seems any need to recapitulate here the good results it brings, both directly and indirectly, in terms of human relations in the factory. Table 2, "Intangible Benefits of the QC Circle Movement" is taken from *QC for the Foreman,* no. 29, in the hope that it may be of use. There, many members mentioned that they "had gained confidence in (their) work."

Human resource development for the future of the enterprise

In summary, I would like to quote a passage from "Quality is the Barometer of Entrepreneurial Reality," an article by Katsuyoshi Ishihara of Matsushita Electric Industrial Co., in *QC for the Foreman,* no. 54.

"In examining standards by which entrepreneurial ability has been measured, we have passed the day of sales as a criterion and are now in a period where profitability is foremost. In all likelihood, however, the standard of the future will be the availability of human resources.

"Within this context, the QC Circle emphasizes increasing the leadership and supervisory capacity of first-line supervisors, and carrying out the requisite educational programs. It is also concerned with training all personnel in the development of an autonomous and spontaneous awareness of quality and associated problems, in order to effect practical application in the shop.

"This all ties in with human resource development, and it will be apparent that the QC Circle is equally important to the future development of the enterprise."

Questionnaire

	No.	Per cent
How did you feel when you first joined the QC Circle?		
Wanted to study	24	63
Was invited	14	37
Was not invited	0	0
Only joined because of pressure	0	0
Total	38	100
Do you attend the circle meetings?		
Attend regularly	33	86
Attend occasionally	4	11
Have never attended	0	0
No answer	1	3
Total	38	100
What about the atmosphere at meetings?		
Stiff and formal	11	29
Pleasant and friendly	22	57
Undirected and disorganized	1	3
No answer	4	11
Total	38	100
What, if anything, needs to be done to improve the atmosphere?		
Fine as it is	23	61
Discipline should be tightened	3	6
Discipline should be relaxed	10	26
No answer	2	5
Total	38	100

What do you think of the agenda of meetings up to now?

Satisfactory	35	92
Difficult to understand	1	3
Useless	2	5
Total	38	100

What are your ideas for the agenda of future meetings?

No particular change required	20	53
Take up more specialized topics	7	18
More emphasis on the company as a whole	10	26
No answer	1	3
Total	38	100

What do you think of exchanges with other plants?

Should be actively pursued	5	13
Premature considering actual conditions	11	29
A good idea if only occasionally	16	42
Should put more emphasis on ourselves	6	16
Total	38	100

What should be done with the 50 yen monthly dues?

Purchase of reference publications	25	60
Refreshments to be consumed at meetings	7	16
For an occasional party	9	21
No answer	1	3
Total	42	100

Movement

Self-confidence, pride, ability, reliability
1. Developed the gumption to solve problems without assistance from others.
2. Developed confidence that the workers can solve any problem by themselves.
3. Far from just giving up on rejects as a problem that just had to be lived with, (we) developed confidence in our ability to pick up the threads that would lead to a solution.
4. Employees developed reliance in QC and tendered their cooperation.
5. Developed an appreciation of the value of work itself.
6. Developed the ability of self-expression.
7. Improved ability to do things alone.

Self-education
1. The shop employees' drive for self-improvement spread beyond QC, so that they spontaneously began the study of other topics, too.
2. Foremen came to see problems in a larger perspective.
3. Hitherto unknown skills were mastered.
4. Personal growth resulted from the long term group educational activities.

Leadership
1. Greater confidence was instilled in the attitude of supervisors towards their duties.
2. It was keenly felt that whether the willingness and responsibility of workers developed or not was influenced by the diligence of the supervisors with whom they were in daily contact.
3. Foremen became more competent in their grasping of leadership.
4. Supervisory capacity of foremen increased.
5. Foremen came to provide more forceful direction of the work.

Willingness, responsibility
1. Improvement in the supervisory system clarified each worker's area of responsibility and raised the level of awareness of problems.
2. It became possible to pinpoint the source of difficulties.
3. The status quo was successfully broken and the will to work continued to burn brightly.
4. Worker morale increased and they became more diligent and active in their attitude toward work.
5. Everyone began to approach his work more creatively, suggesting many avenues of improvement.
6. Awareness developed that work standards must undergo continuous improvement.
7. The level of self-supervision was raised.

QC awareness
1. QC spread to the farthest corner of the factory, and everyone developed consciousness of quality, costs, problems, and improvements.

2. The increase in QC consciousness improved morale.
3. Competitiveness in the best sense encouraged cost reductions.
4. Everyone began on his own to supervise and check himself, even without nagging, so that the level of quality automatically rose.

Communication
1. Information became freely available, so that positive measures could be quickly taken.
2. Things that had heretofore been done by intuition were now perceived through graphs and Pareto diagrams. Thus conditions were grasped and information feedback became available.
3. Relations with executive superiors and with those involved in preceding or following processes underwent marked improvement.
4. Appreciation of the other fellow's point of view was engendered, and exchange of opinion was facilitated.
5. Everyone became able to speak out frankly.

Teamwork
1. Whenever a problem arose, everyone pulled together to improve quality.
2. Immediacy was brought to the feeling that QC Circles were basic to the problem-solving process.
3. The savour of QC activities was appreciated and a system of over-all cooperation became regularized.
4. Both workers and foremen pitched in together, and QC commanded universal cooperation and participation.
5. The cooperative activities of the circles cemented human relations.

Factory environment
1. Standardization resulted in the elimination of excessive demands on workers, waste, and inconsistencies. Work became easier and the shop a more pleasant place.
2. The number of workers shirking their regular duties decreased, constructive discussion and suggestions increased, and corrective advice was accepted with a cooperative attitude.
3. Human relations improved, the factory was happier, and employees developed a positive attitude.

Scientific thinking
1. Education brought out the ability to appraise a question from a number of angles.
2. Problems were presented statistically, and important problems could be pinpointed for solution.
3. Foremen could make use of factual data to lend strength to their directives.
4. Control techniques by the 'Deming Cycle' (Plan-Do-Check-Act) were worked out in full.

Perfection of policy and planning
1. The foremen in the shops were integrated in the over-all QC plans of the establishment, so that the policies of the president or plant manager were completed to the final level.
2. Control items and area of responsibility were clarified for each worker, completing the control system.
3. Control came to be carried out without fail.
4. Employer-employee relations improved.

QC Circle activities and implementation of QC techniques

Taro Ihara*

QC Circle and techniques
Japan's QC Circles are already world famous. One of the factors that led to such great development of the movement, which began in 1962, is in the author's opinion, that instead of remaining just another activity for building morale, it extended, in line with the basic philosophy of quality control, to actual exercise of a control function based on solid data.

In other words, the movement developed so well because the leaders and members of the circles studied the ideals and techniques of quality control and applied them in their shops.

What, then, are the techniques used by QC Circles? The results of a survey taken at a Bridgestone Tire factory are shown in figure 1.

While it is said that over 80 per cent of the problems confronting the circles can be solved by simple techniques, this is not to say that the remaining techniques should be classed as complex. Indeed, they are more than familiar to any QC Circle.

Brief technical explanations of some of the more representative techniques are given below.

Key QC techniques
1 Pareto diagrams
Figure 1, which is itself a Pareto diagram, shows that Pareto diagrams are the most common method used by QC Circles, accounting for over 30 per cent of all QC charts used by them. Cause-and-effect are the second commonest method. Our definition may then be that anything that separates the elements of question

---

* Mr Ihara is Manager, Quality Control Section, Tokyo Plant, Bridgestone Tire Co., Kodaira City, Tokyo.

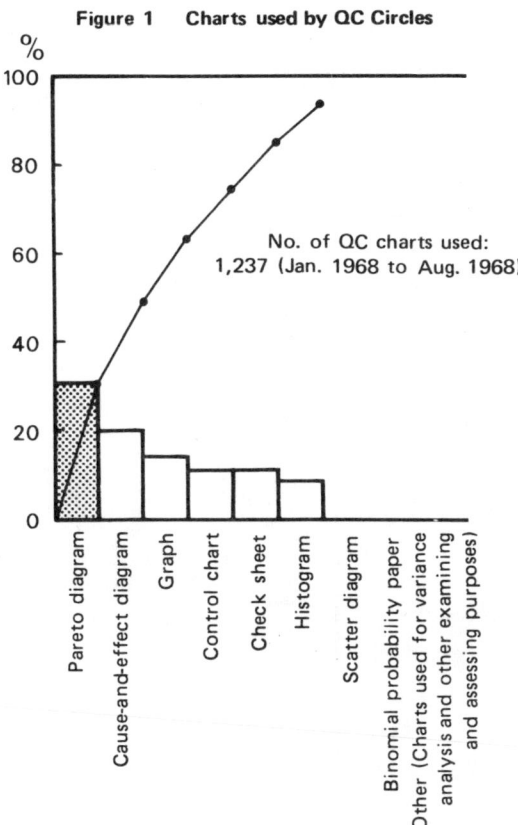

Figure 1 Charts used by QC Circles

No. of QC charts used: 1,237 (Jan. 1968 to Aug. 1968)

and indicates their approximate relative importance may be called a Pareto diagram.

Such slogans as 'Use Pareto diagrams to set improvement targets' and 'Use Pareto diagrams to check effectiveness of improvements' are often heard, but as in anything else it is first necessary to put things in perspective. We must not fall between two stools. The key to success is to avoid the dissipation of effort and concentrate all problem-solving capabilities on a single target.

Furthermore, if you're going to have a target, it may as well be a vital one. Rather than hunting down many trivial causes of rejected work, concentration on the most vital cause will require less manpower and be more effective.

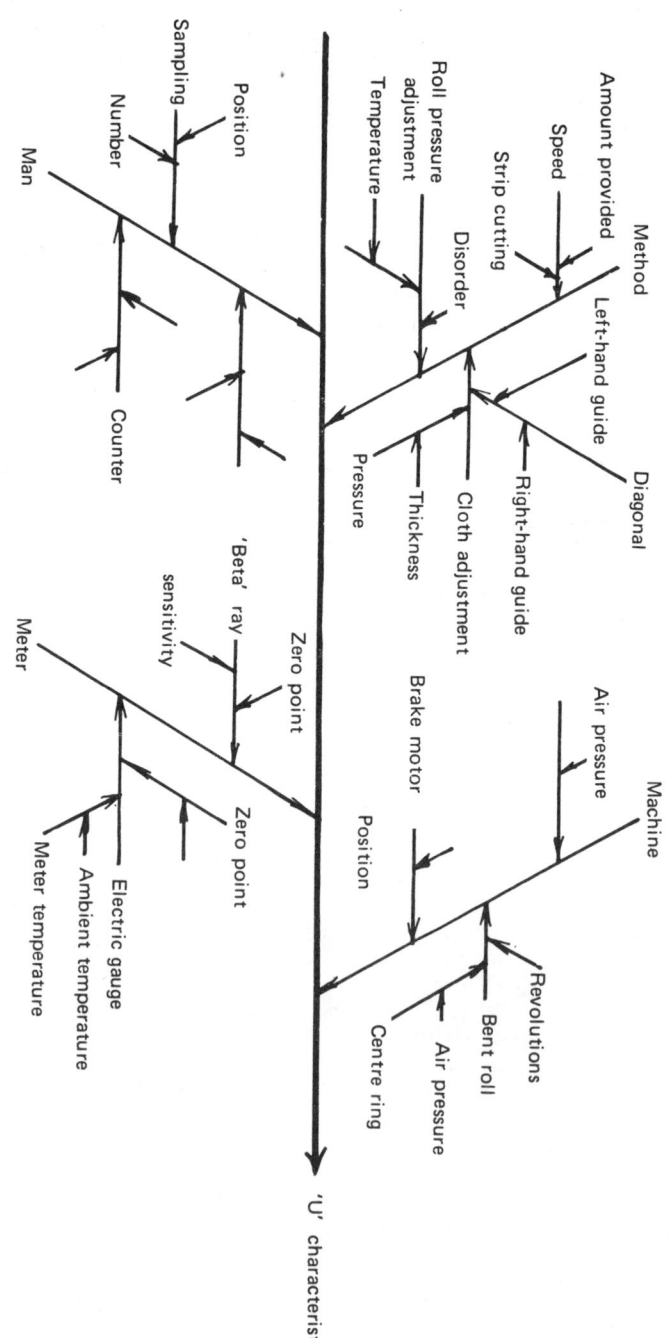

Figure 2 Example of a cause-and-effect diagram

QC CIRCLE ACTIVITIES AND QC TECHNIQUES

2 Cause-and-effect diagrams

In solving problems, it is necessary to have a clear view of your target. That is, once you have found from the Pareto diagram what to attack, and have decided to begin, you must find out what the causes of the target error or defects, etc are.

It must be discovered what causes produce what effects.

The discovery of these causes and effects, often called data analysis, involves the use of cause-and-effect diagrams. Figure 2 shows this relationship between the resultant performance and the various causes in a 'fish bone' form.

In this case, use is often made of the combined force of many minds by 'brainstorming,' since, as the proverb has it, 'two heads are better than one.'

Here, I would like to make two point. One is that brainstorming involves a group of people who fire off a series of accusations at the factor which each thinks is behind the problem. But the 'suspects' which emerge at this stage are no more than that. The 'criminal' is still to be found. Thus, it is still necessary to get down to facts and data in terms of black and white.

The second point is interconnected. It is definitely not enough to just draw up the diagram and let it go at that. As the level of data analysis in the factory rises and more and more problems are identified, it will be necessary to erase unnecessary causes and add new ones, in order to develop a standardized catalogue of causes.

What the group finally succeeds in formulating, then, is only the first stage diagram, and only by crossing out and adding, in a continuing process of polishing, can a factory's essential improvements be made. Thus, the 'cause-and-effect diagram' is an excellent indicator of level of technological and control sophistication.

3 Control charts

As indicated by such often-heard expressions as 'QC begins and ends with control charts' or 'the statistical quality control (SQC) of a factory *is* control charts,' this device is central to factory QC techniques.

It is well known that however much you try to equalize manufacturing conditions, there will be deviations from standards and specifications in the finished products. However, we may consider that there are 'unavoidable' or allowable deviations, i.e. those which fall within a certain range, barring accidents, and 'avoidable' deviations, which are beyond that range.

The control chart, by setting the upper and lower limits of deviations, is essential in that it allows us to find out whether production is stabilized or not, and to control the productive process.

There are several kinds of control charts: the 'X-R' type which shows data by variables, the 'P' type which indicates data by attributes on a 'go or no-go' (accept or not-accept) basis, the 'C' type which gives, say the number of defects per unit area, and others. Figure 3 is of the X-R type and shows the width of an intermediate material.

As far as details for developing and using control charts are concerned, the reader is referred to existing examples, but from my experience in discussing and advising QC Circle members on these charts and related data, I venture to mention the following points.

1 Control charts are easy to draw up but hard to use.
2 Whether a chart can be put to use depends on the diligence and patience of the user.
3 Control charts cannot be used in isolation. Such peripheral devices as cause-and-effect diagrams, emergency procedure standards and production standard objectives must be fitted into a clear-cut over-all relationship.
4 It is necessary to have digested knowledge about grouping and stratification of data.

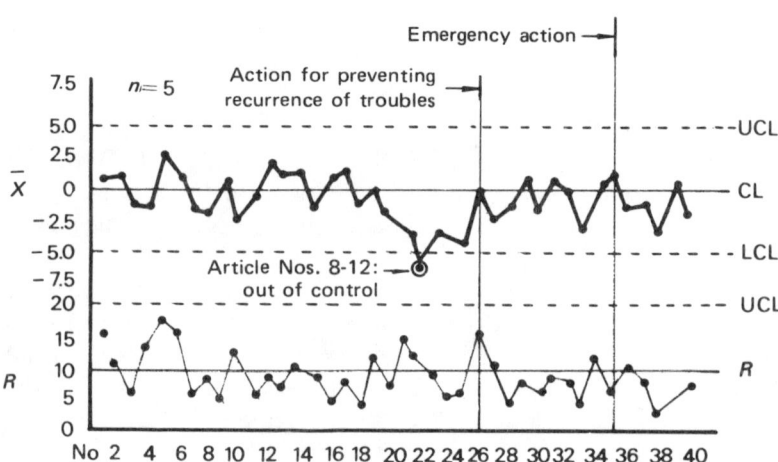

Figure 3   Control chart for the width of 'PC' material

QC CIRCLE ACTIVITIES AND QC TECHNIQUES

5 In tackling a characteristic, it is necessary to limit your controlling capability to what you can manage yourself, otherwise there is no hope of success.

4 Check sheets

If a system is in operation where data can be easily gathered in the factory and is automatically translated into easy-to-use form, the action which can be taken will be productive of results. The check sheet is made with this object in mind. It is designed to be easily visible and instantly perceivable as a whole.

The example shown in figure 4 deals with reason for rejects, and it can be seen at a glance that these are most prevalent on the old machines, and then, in the afternoon.

Besides the foregoing, there are, as in the case of the histograms to be taken up next, a variety of types. Some show division of defect causes and others are for checking, by the workers, of each cause of defects, to provide a final check on inspection procedures.

Figure 4 Check sheet of defects

Machine	Worker's experience	Monday		Tuesday		Wednesday		Thursday		Friday		Saturday		Total		Total
		A.M.	P.M.	A.M.	P.M.	A.M.	P.M.	A.M.	P.M.	A.M.	P.M.	A.M.	P.M.	A.M.	P.M.	
Old type	Eight years	o	ooo xx△	ox	△△x	oxx	oxx △△	ox	oox xx△	oo	oxx △△	ooo x	ox△ △△	14	30	44
	Two years	oox	oox △△	oox	oxx △	oox x	△△ △	△△△	oxx △△		△△x xx	oxx o	oxx △△	17	28	45
New type	Six years	o△	x	△	oxx	ox△	ox	ox	△	oo	ox△	ooo x	ox△ △	15	14	29
	Two years	xx		ox	o	o△△	oo	△x	o	o	x	o△△	oo	13	7	20
	Total	8	12	8	'11	13	13	9	13	6	14	15	16	59	79	138

o ..... Looseness   x ..... Scratches   △ ..... Breakage

Figure 5   Histogram for the weight of 'T' material for work in progress

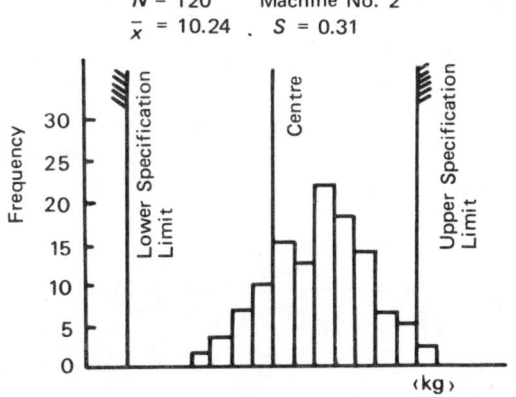

5 Histograms

Figure 5 shows a histogram of the weight of an intermediate product in a process. From it, we can see that the intermediate product in question is a little heavy, and that there is a rather wide deviation from the centre.

Histograms thus bring out a data distribution showing a central tendency and whether the data are within the standard deviation. If they do not satisfy our requirements, separate histograms should be prepared through stratification of data on workers, machines and materials, and when the cause becomes apparent countermeasures should be taken.

Occasionally, a basic renovation of plant, equipment and working procedure may be required but as this will increase costs, the institution of inspection procedures is a feasible alternative. As in the case of the Pareto diagram, a comparison must be made with data before and after the attempt at improvement in order to confirm its effectiveness. It is therefore essential to form the habit of noting the date on which data for any histogram was collected. There should be at least 30, and usually from 50 to 100 data items.

6 Scatter diagrams

There is always the question of the relationship between any two phenomena. Examples are whether conveyor speed influences the defective product rate or the percentage of constituent A influences product breakage.

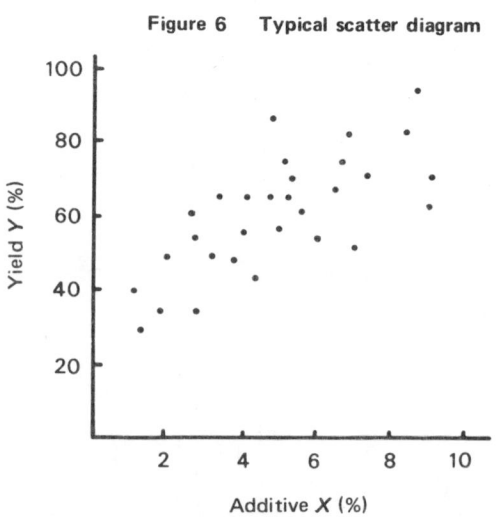

Figure 6   Typical scatter diagram

QC CIRCLE ACTIVITIES AND QC TECHNIQUES

With the exception of the cause-and-effect diagram, all the methods heretofore discussed have dealt with problems related to a single performance value, but here we wish to take up the relationship between two sets of data. Here, however, it is necessary that both of these sets of data be capable of application.

Figure 6 is a scatter diagram showing the relationship between percentage of a certain additive and the yield of the product. It shows that when the amount of additive is increased, yield increases.

Generally the data which is thought to represent the cause is placed on the vertical axis of the diagram and the assumed effect on the horizontal. The presence or absence of a relationship may be calculated in index form, or more simply, by the use of a median, but just drawing the diagram is sufficient to give a general indication.

7 Binomial probability sheets

When there is a question, as in figure 4, of differences in rejection rates between new and old machines, binomial probability paper is used in measuring data by attributes. However, it is also used when the data can be converted into data by variables and measured in plus and minus or ordinal values, making it an exceedingly widely applicable technique. Limitations of space preclude anything more than the presentation of figure 7, but the figure can be used widely for process analysis. Thus, if everyone is always ready to make immediate use of this, it can be of immense assistance.

Figure 7 Typical sampling inspection by use of a binomial probability sheet

Do Companies A and B have different acceptance rates?

	Acceptable lots	Rejected lots	Total
Company A	86	2	88
Company B	44	8	52
Total	130	10	140

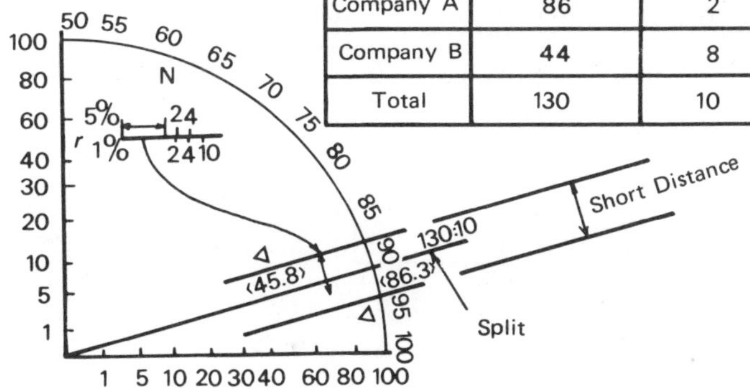

QUALITY CONTROL CIRCLE CASE STUDIES

8 Graphs

It is of course true that the Pareto diagrams, histograms, and control charts already taken up are within the meaning of the word 'graph.' However, the term is used in figure 1 to indicate graphs which are not included in any of these categories.

There are many kinds of graphs — line, bar, circle, etc — but one is always prone to wonder, when looking at a factory's graph, what it is attempting to show and how it can be put to use.

Since the graph is a visual means of presentation, it is capable of imparting information more quickly than the table with its row upon row of digits. It is also necessary in view of the energy spent in drawing the graph, to keep one from simply enjoying the visual appeal and being content with only that.

There are analytical, control, planning, cumulative, statistical and other types of graphs, each with its own uses. Since there is no space to give examples of all of them, we will content ourselves the writer's factory and which aims at finding an average (x) and a standard deviation (sigma).

Figure 8 Graph for calculation of average x and standard deviation (y)

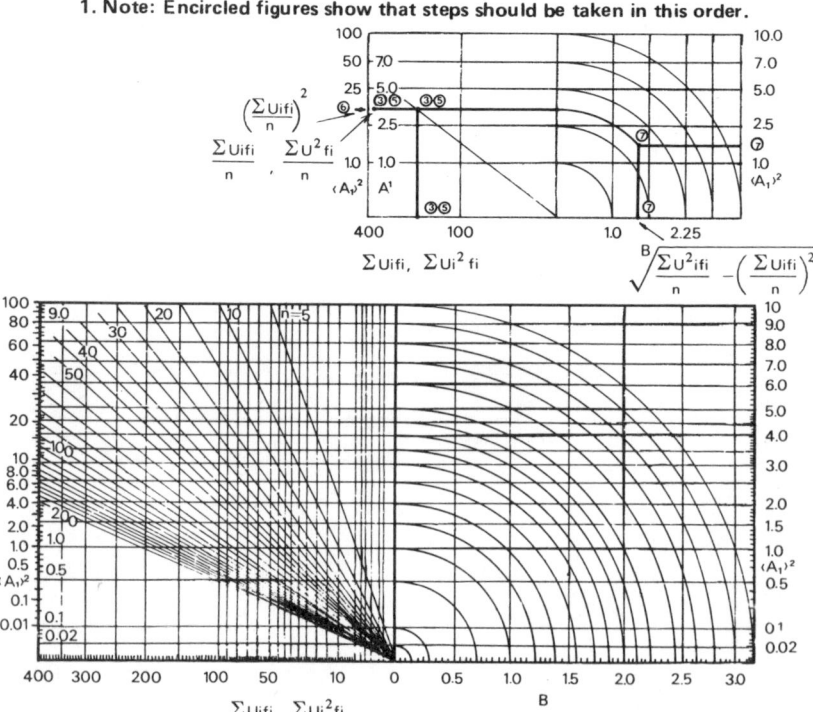

1. Note: Encircled figures show that steps should be taken in this order.

Summary

In the writer's factory, QC Circles were formed at about the end of 1964. At first, the only means employed were Pareto diagrams, cause-and-effect diagrams, graphs, and histograms. Of course, it was still possible to solve quite a number of problems and increase effectiveness; but the circle leaders and members began to undertake actual study in the factory in addition to the educational programmes planned and carried out by the factory—they started to buy, of their own accord, such foreman-directed magazines as *QC for the Foreman* and *QC Textbook for Foremen* and other publications, established study groups, initiated self-help activities, and eventually became able to handle the more sophisticated techniques. The improvements brought about by implementing these techniques gave the circle new confidence and appreciation of the value of their contribution. At the same time, these activities provided the means whereby the control activities of the shop were gradually formulated. Thus, executives, who formerly were overloaded with trouble-shooting duties, became free to devote themselves to more forward-looking managerial activities.

The seven items used by the writer's company in employee training in quality control are data stratification, control points, control charts, histograms, Pareto diagrams, cause-and-effect diagrams and scatter diagrams. But as can be understood from the often heard remark that "quality control lies in deviation demarcation and data stratification," it is these two that are most often important in examining any situation. We also take the following five slogans as the basis of these methods and try to mold our thoughts and actions accordingly. They are:

1. Get the PDCA (Plan-Do-Check-Act) habit.
2. Activate the 5 Ws and 1H (What, Why, Where, When, Who and How).
3. Push actively for standardization.
4. Put things in data form.
5. Control the crucial factors.

The thing I wish to emphasize in closing is the overwhelming importance of basing utilization of techniques on these ideas, and of laying a solid structure of ideas on this basic foundation.

The QC Circle and training

Katsuyoshi Ishihara*

The beginnings of QC Circles

1 Magazine provides stimulus

First of all, it is necessary to realize that it was the publication of the monthly *QC for the Foreman* in April, 1962, which brought about the birth of the QC Circles.

Prior to the start of publication, great thought was given to the problem of how the magazine could be used to fuel first-line factory activities in quality control, and several decisions were taken: to edit the magazine for first-line supervisory personnel; to make it low in price, and to use the magazine as an instrument to promote the formation of QC Circles.

These are the policies that lay at the beginnings of Japan's unique QC Circles.

We must not forget the respect and gratitude we owe to those people who developed these policies and provided leadership to industry.

2 QC Circle objectives

The headquarters of the QC Circle movement sets out the following aims and objectives for the circles:

1. To develop leadership and control ability in first echelon supervisors, and to encourage their self-development.
2. To raise shop morale, including that of all the employees, and to maintain a spontaneously generated awareness of quality, of attendant problems, and of the possibilities of improvement in order that quality control can be carried through to the ultimate degree.

---

*Mr Ishihara is Manager of the Controls Engineering Department, Parts Depot, Matsushita Electric Industrial Co., Kadoma City, Osaka Prefecture.

3   To become the focus in each shop for the firm's overall QC activities, and to take an effective role in putting across the chairman's or plant manager's plans, in fixing control procedures in the shop, and in assuring quality standards.

The author feels that for the executive it is most important, first of all, to understand these objectives, and then to analyze the abilities of foremen and operators in order to work out and put into practice a plan of action which matches the situations in that company.

A QC Circle will not last long if it is brought into being without an understanding of its significance and objectives, and an appreciation of the place of the circle in the company-wide QC picture.

In order to get a viable QC Circle, the enthusiasm of the foremen and workers under them must be neatly balanced by interest and diligent application by executives. Only then can the circle become a nucleus of lively QC activity. When managers and executives are just bystanders, success can hardly be expected.·

Three forms of QC Circle training

1   Self-development through QC Circle activities
As has been mentioned, the origins and objectives of the circles begin with study groups centred on first echelon supervisors. I feel that the encouragement of on-the-job training within the circles is in keeping with the ideas of self-development.

I further feel that when this attitude is applied to the circles' training activities, the following problems arise: (1) Personnel at the managerial level must construct a base on which the circles can develop actively, and must make clear the position of the circles within the company as a whole. They must keep a fatherly eye on the various self-development programmes, and maintain an attitude of extremely strong interest. They must be quick to praise, and must make official announcements and awards. (2) Middle management must organize study groups, exchange seminars and conferences for the evaluation of material studied in the circles; that is, assume a promotional role. Besides the obvious duty of assisting in leadership, they must also be tireless in their efforts to remove anything which might impede their subordinates' progress in self-improvement. (3) The members must correctly appreciate the purposes of activities, and through them strive towards full development of both leaders and members.

If QC Circle activities are carried on in line with the following methods, self-improvement will proceed smoothly.

Do not become active only when a problem is discovered. Rather, keep things going at a pace for day-to-day self-study, training and action.

Cases are seen where circle activities are encouraged in the direction of suggesting improvements or raising quality, where the group is formed anew for each problem. Leading the circle in this way makes it possible that after a long period of looking inward, there will arise self-improvement of the group itself.

It is also important to lead the circle in such a way that independence and spontaneity are encouraged, and discussions are carried out about each members' responsibilities for control items and failures. The whole group should think and study together.

The achievement of this independence and spontaneity is one of the points of industrial education, and from this point of view it may well be said that QC Circle activities are an opportunity for education and training.

One of the good points of training in the circles is that education is not viewed as something separated from work but as training, independently achieved through actual experience.

In the sense of providing training through experience, it is essential that the circle take up problems of intimate concern to the shop. A few samples of points to be considered here are: personnel's self-evaluation of their performance in the shop; ideas on how to achieve rationalization; complaints and people's views on workers up and down the line; ideas on rejects; discussions and suggestions about production volume, delivery dates, costs, and other immediate problems.

It can also be said that to organize meetings in cooperation with other circles, to set a theme for exchange factory visits and to strive toward mutual improvement are examples of practical studies. Attending conferences and exchange-of-experience meetings, within and outside of the company and taking part in the discussions are also very effective in the direction of self-improvement.

1 Mutual development is enhanced by holding 'announcement of experience meetings' within the firm. These should always be in close consultation with managers and executives, who should take care not to dampen the enthusiasm of the leader. They should search for a way to praise even the most ill-considered report,

seeking out the good points and agreeing with them. On these occasions, such expressions as "I venture to hope that . . ." are extremely important in pointing out problems.
2   Exchange meetings with other circles, both within and outside the company may be held for mutual improvement. It must not be forgotten that exchange meetings are living opportunities for study. By taking the most pressing problem as a theme, the exchange meeting can be made down-to-earth and fruitful.
3   QC Circle forums and conferences should be held for the shop, section or factory in order to keep a check on activities. Superiors may utilize the occasions to single out deserving personnel for awards or commendation.
4   One should obtain a broad grasp of activities in other companies and, as the best means of raising one's own circle level, take part in QC Circle conferences and foremen's QC conferences sponsored by QC Circle Headquarters, as well as in the activities of regional QC Circle branches.

2   Actual example of training within the industry
Although the circles have a training function, it is still true that without a full understanding of QC techniques, it will be difficult for the circle to function smoothly. To solve this problem, the author recommends the following basic QC-oriented educational activities.

One company has developed a foremen's QC course as the heart of their QC Circle leader programme. This utilizes actual experiences in each shop, encourages activities and enlivens circle organization. This method is briefly introduced below.

Objectives of education and training: I feel it essential that, once training plans are formulated and carried out, they should not be allowed to end with mere mastery of knowledge and techniques; but, rather, be at the bottom, diffused throughout the daily activities by means of an approach to the major problems within the organization and centred on the trainees. Concrete aims of this training are: Cultivation of human resources and attitudes; adoption of scientific control techniques adapted to the capabilities of the leaders; and encouragement of the idea that the most important point is contributing to managerial achievement through scientifically grounded control techniques and activities.

The education system and its planning: In actually carrying out an education and training programme, it is necessary first to establish a plan and then progress on the basis of a 'check-act' cycle. This plan must be based on the over-all system, and must keep a close relationship to encouraging the QC Circle and management policy, and must satisfy the requirements of both. This is a most important point.

The distinguishing feature of this course is that it formulates a network which reaches from educational planning to the confirmation of results on a controlled daily schedule, and aims at a thorough-going programme of on-the-job training for executives, participants, members and subordinates. Aims and procedures of this course are given below:

Aims of the course are (1) to teach participants to use simple QC techniques and apply them to actual problems, thus raising efficiency, and (2) by assigning actual topics and instilling ability to take proper action, to strengthen the functioning of QC Circles.

Procedures are summarized in table 1. Additional details follow.

Time: from 9 a.m. to 4 p.m. every day for six days (36 course hours). After the course ends, a meeting is held once a month to study actual activity. One week before the training, a 90-minute preparatory session is held to underscore the aims and procedure of the training.

Target personnel: Foremen and alternates in the first supervisory echelon, i.e. the QC Circle leaders.

Number of participants: 30-50 per course.

Site: Conference rooms inside the company.

Methods: lectures, exercises, assignments, examinations, questionnaires, study of actual practice, slide shows.

Exercises are given in each subject based on actual data and information from the factory. Assignments are given in each subject and participants are selected at random to report. They discuss the thoughts and analyses presented to deepen the understanding of the participants. Daily assignments are given to deepen understanding of each subject. These should be devised by the instructors, their assistants, and office staff. Reported assignments should be reviewed by an education committee and forwarded to the office by the appointed day. Subjects which involve assignments are frequency distribution, control charts, and binomial probability sheets. The content of examinations are drawn from the sixth days' lectures for objective evaluation of individual ability. Questions can be true-and-false, multiple choice, fill-in-the-blanks, matching or computational types. In questionnaires, the participants should be asked whether the standard of instruction was good, what improvements, if any, can be made in the course, and whether the content, methods and length of the course were suitable or not. For study of actual practice, the QC techniques learned in the lectures are put to practical use, with the participants and instructors discussing problems in their shops. Results should be obtained within three months. Opportunities are provided for practical activities in the shop and to carry out activities in an organized manner in the QC Circle. To get an accurate check on results, checks are made and instruction offered on the activities of the shop every month. Slides may be shown on the following topics to give final form to material learned in lectures, and to make the material more effective: outline of quality control (supervisors and QC); how to collect and process data; control charts; and the discovery and solutions of quality problems. Overhead projectors are used to supplement the educational methods employed in the lectures and exercises. Notations may be freely made on the material to be projected, and any number may be projected together for analysis, giving greater educational impact.

Encouragement of practical study and training: As has already been pointed out, education and training in the QC Circle aims at improving the participants, putting their new knowledge to work in daily factory activity, enabling agressive clarification and solution of problems and, thus, achieving results which contribute to higher profits. The personality, ability, and aptitude of each participant is different. There will be those who can absorb the content of the training programme and those who cannot.

With such a varied group, one of the most essential points is to give everyone a chance to develop his own individual abilities to the utmost. This will be effective in combining education and training to most fully bring out the many-faceted abilities of the participants.

A full appreciation of this line of reasoning has led one company to institute a unique post-course follow-up system consisting of practical study meetings centred on the participants where topics are selected for emphasis and organized attention is given to encouragement.

The structure of practical study meetings may be described as

THE QC CIRCLE AND TRAINING

Table 1 Content and schedule of the education and training system

Day	Subject	Content	Objective	Hours
First	What is Quality Control?	Definition, history, and present situation of QC; What is 'quality' and 'control'; how to control quality.	To give a grasp of the outlines of QC.	
	QC for first-line supervisors	Role of first-line supervisors, what are control items, ten rules for successful shop QC, standardization of work procedures.	To teach the QC aspect of supervisor's duties.	3
	Slide show	An outline of quality control (supervisors and QC).		
	Pareto diagram	How to make, read, and use Pareto diagrams (with exercises).	To inculcate awareness of the importance of this tool in discovering problems.	
	Cause-and-effect diagram	Definition of cause-and-effect diagrams, and the relationship between performance and cause (including exercises).	To obtain a realization of this tool as a check on the relationship between the problem and the cause.	3
Second	Frequency distribution	Statistical treatment of data; definition of frequency distribution and how to chart it.	To show the necessity of taking statistical view of data, and to provide techniques to achieve this.	3
	Frequency distribution	How to make things (exercises), how to read and use frequency distribution charts and how to statistically represent distribution.		3
	Slide show	How to collect and process data.		
Third	Control chart	Definition; how to make control charts of data by variables (with exercises).	To achieve s situation where the control chart can be used effectively as a means for controlling manufacturing processes (process improvement, process control).	3
	Control chart	How to make control charts of data by attributes (with exercises), how to read them, and their usefulness.		3
	Slide show	What are control charts.		
Fourth	Binomial probability sheet	Inspection and estimation using data by variables (with exercises).	To provide a grasp of techniques for making statistical judgment of the various pre-requisites in a manufacturing process.	3
	Binomial probability sheet	Inspection and estimation using data by attributes (with exercises).		
Fifth	Process control	Definition of the process, how to unearth its problems and solve them.	To provide a grasp of techniques of analyzing, improving, and controlling manufacturing processes.	3
	Study of actual examples			
	Process improvement Study of actual examples	Definition of process control.		3
Sixth	Review exercises	Have one of the participants give answers to each of the assignments and deepen understanding through discussion	Conduct practice exercises based on each of the subjects in order to deepen the understanding of the participants.	3
	Examinations		To check the level of understanding of the participants.	1
	Evaluation			

follows. These meetings are the forum in which general guidance is given on the direction, procedure, and methods of analysis to be followed for a specific period of time, such as three months. This is organized activity, carried on within the QC Circle framework.

Table 2 shows a system which may be recommended for assisting and improving these activities.

Practical activities regarding important topics centred on those who recently finished the training course for the foremen begin by developing a 'practical study activity system.' In choosing the topics, one must choose important points so that activity results in concrete achievements.

Evaluation of education and training is a rather difficult process in many ways, but the method used should be to check whether the results obtained are in line with objectives, and if the educational programme is bearing fruit, by convening a form in which superiors and various involved parties can confirm these results ('result announcement meeting').

Another use of the practical activities is to bring out the strengths and weaknesses of personnel (creativity, understanding, diligence, sense of responsibility, aptitude in applying techniques, adaptability, etc). An example of evaluating education and training activities is presented in the table below. Concerning lecture conditions (understanding), the degree to which the trainees understood the content of the lectures and other problems involving the trainees, basic ability, adaptability, and understanding, as well as the content of the lectures and the suitability of the scheduling must be grasped. Concerning practical activity, what must

Table 2 Participants of practical study groups

Participants	Remarks
Chief instructor	From outside (JUSE)
Chief company instructor	A factory technical department manager or a QC section chief
Company instructors	Six or eight men — QC section chiefs or those who finished the basic QC course
Executives directly above those recently trained in the course	
Middle management	Plant or department managers
Trainees	
Task force, QC Circle members	Members of organizations for action centred around the topics of the course trainees

be determined is the degree to which each trainee was able to apply the ideals and techniques of quality control which he had learned to the topics selected, initiate activity in cooperation with other groups, and whether concrete results were achieved (table 3). Table 3 is an example of an educational programme for circle leaders. But if it is desired that the circle be a forum for independent and spontaneous study through shop control and improvement campaigns, I feel it is most valuable, for the enterprise as

Table 3 Practical activity evaluation

Topic	Basis for evaluation
Examinations (for trainees)	An average mark of: 81 — 100 good 61 — 80 average 60 or less bad Note particularly distribution and monthly changes in grade (up or down).
Assignments	Percentage handed in: 90% or more good 80 — 90% average 80% or less bad Correctly done assignments (% of those handed in): 80% or more good 80% average 80% or less bad
Attendance	Perfect average One or more absences poor (counting two times late or early departure as one absence)
Questionnaire	Aggregate responses: 80% or more favourable good 60 — 80% " average 60% or less " poor Take note of details in each category.
Progress of practical activity topics	Topic progress (Achievement of Monthly Progress Plan): 90% or more good 80 — 90% average 80% or less poor Percentage of reports on practical activities submitted: On all occasions good Late once average Not submitted once poor
Practical activity study groups	Attendance: Perfect average One absence poor Participation by executives and direct superiors: Perfect attendance good 2 absences average 3 absences poor Number of QC Circle meetings: 6 or more good 4 — 5 average 3 or less poor Attendance of active members at meetings: 80% good 60 — 70% average 60% or less poor Note: At least 50,000 yen (US$140) should be the monthly goal to be saved as a result of practical activity.

well, that a specific programme of education for the leaders be aggressively carried forward.

Further, if it is desired to develop truly superior circle leaders and if concrete results are to be expected of those who complete the training, executives must not excuse themselves because of 'pressure of other duties,' or 'absence of suitable persons.' It is only by providing these opportunities offered by their presence that persons of independent mind can be developed.

3   Use of outside educational facilities

Companies that do not have their own training system may find it convenient to avail themselves of the QC courses for foremen offered by organizations experienced in extra-company education such as the Union of Japanese Scientists and Engineers or the Japan Standards Association.

It often happens that foremen become strongly motivated and attend such courses regularly, particularly because it is so seldom that they have a chance of obtain outside training. It may also be thought valuable to use the emotional lift resulting from being selected in getting them to attend these lectures.

The point to be careful of in such cases is that outside courses tend to be rather passive. In other words, when the participants return to their company after the courses, follow-up activities must be given full attention.

In shops fortunate enough to have a forum for activity in the form of a QC Circle, the importance of a place created by executive personnel in which organized application of the newly learned material is possible becomes apparent.

Let us here introduce, in table 4, from the curriculum of such a course, the foremen's course of the JUSE.

Making use of the techniques learned through training

Due to limitations of space, it is impossible to treat this subject in detail, but I feel confident in saying that the defect of previous training programmes was their emphasis on the acquisition of knowledge alone, and their neglect of its practical application.

As I emphasized in the section on outside training, the independent organizational structure represented by the QC Circles offers an opportunity for practical application. It is most valuable to aggressively progress on the basis of this organization, and fully utilize the various techniques to get concrete results.

In other words, it is most desirable to operate the circles in a way that techniques and scientific methods are correctly applied.

THE QC CIRCLE AND TRAINING

Table 4 Contents of an outside seminar

Day	Lecture Topic	Content	Hours
First	Opening remarks Orientation What is QC — a statistical view (1)	Objectives; organization, etc. of the seminar. Histograms and Pareto diagrams (including ideas on quality testing).	3
	Exercises (1) Foremen's role	Histograms and Pareto diagrams. QC and foremen's part.	3
Second	Statistical view (2)	Graphs, check sheets, frequency distribution charts, calculation of 'sigma,' uses of numerical table (finding of square roots)	3
	Exercises (2) Work standards; Study and discussion (1)	Calculation of 'sigma,' uses of numerical tables and scatter diagrams.	5
Third	Process improvement (1)	What is process improvement; where is the problem; how to find the problem and decide on the target of attack; data stratification and cause-and-effect diagrams.	3
	Exercises (3) Process improvement (2)	Cause-and-effect diagrams. How to determine the target of attack, how to judge effectiveness, how to carry on day-to-day process control.	3
Fourth	Control charts (1)	What are control charts; how to draw them (1) (including the $\bar{x}$-R chart).	3
	Exercises (4) Inspection	$\bar{x}$-R control chart. What is inspection; sampling inspection.	3
Fifth	Control charts (1) (numerical values)	How to draw control charts (2) ('U' chart may be omitted); how to read and use control charts (how to find the upper and lower control on the 'n' number of values.	3
	Exercises (5) Controls Study and discussion (2)	$\bar{P}$ control chart. How to install controls.	5
Sixth	QC Circle operation	QC Circle functioning and related problems.	3
	Assurance of quality Question-and-answer session	Based on questions from the participants relating to the course as a whole and on problems passed on from the discussions.	3

Future educational activities of QC Circles?

Up until here, my presentation has been centred on QC techniques; but in the future QC Circles will have to move on from this base, that is, proceed from quality improvement and elimination of rejects to increasing operational efficiency (by industrial engineering) and cutting costs (by value engineering), studying to achieve the kind of over-all ability which makes for the kind of supervisor who really can be relied on, in the first echelon of the factory.

To further increase the effectiveness of QC, IE and VE, creativity must be built up. The advantages of the QC group can be enhanced by brainstorming, and the adoption of training in eliciting individual creativity.

Conclusion

Let me sum up the points I have made in connection with QC Circles and training. It is important that managers, supervisors and executives take measures, geared to the level and capabilities of each enterprise, which will respect and move the employees who make up the organization from the basic level of human nature — the social drive and the drive toward self-improvement, and will channel this, in the team or group context, into the management of the enterprise.

Smaller enterprises and QC Circle activities

Akira Harada*

Smaller enterprises from the viewpoint of quality control

There are many yardsticks used to determine just what it is that makes an enterprise 'smaller.' It may be capitalization or it may be sales. One may also measure on the basis of number of employees but staff composition differs from industry to industry, with the result that in some fields a company with only 100 employees qualifies as a large enterprise; while in another, a concern with over a thousand workers is still a 'smaller enterprise.'

Be that as it may, smaller enterprises are the foundation of Japan's present prosperity, and unless they are invested with real strength, no sustained continuation of this prosperity can be expected.

Traditionally, smaller enterprises have been feeble economically, with low per-person productivity, and hourly pay rates far below those of large concerns. Their equipment is outdated, too; but these conditions can be tolerated no longer.

The problem of most vital interest in the management of smaller enterprises is personnel. In the last 10 years, labor costs have rocketed upward, without regard to boom or recession, and it is getting to the point where unless the wages offered are slightly better than those of large companies, the requisite labor cannot be attracted. And in the longer view as well, labor will be a seller's maket for the next 20 years at least, and it will become increasingly difficult to obtain not only young, but even middle-aged and older personnel.

When we consider this continuous rise in the cost of labor coupled with the rapid decline in its quality, it can be seen that

---

*Mr Harada is Technology Department Manager, Auto Radio Division, Matsushita Communication Industrial Co., Yokohama.

unless the smaller enterprises attain technological and productivity levels comparable to those of large companies, their very existence will be jeopardized. Rather, the smaller enterprises of the future must strive to become high-productivity units, while maintaining the characteristic individuality absent in larger enterprises.

As a practical problem, however, smaller enterprises suffer from many disadvantages in comparison to large enterprises. These may be summarized as follows:

1. Their technology is so retarded that they cannot compete in terms of quality.
2. Their economic base is weak, leaving them vulnerable to business fluctuations.
3. They have a tendency to nepotism, so that promotional opportunities are lacking and the development of talent is impeded.
4. Work often progresses by the ability of individuals, at the expense of the organization.
5. There is a tendency to neglect the longer view under the pressure of immediate tasks.
6. It often happens that scientific investigation is subordinated to intuition.
7. If the policy of the parent company or major client changes, or a long-standing contact is replaced, the ramifications can reach the roots of the company's activities and impede independent action.
8. Immediate profit is valued more than long-term gains.
9. No store of expertise is built up, and value is placed on the person who can work neatly and improvise.
10. Such qualities as 'spirit' and 'attitude' are valued above the rational thinking approach.
11. Standards of assessment are not well established, whether in work procedures, personnel, or quality.
12. In times of troubles, there is a tendency to take *ad hoc* action, with little calm reflection, which would lead to measures to prevent recurrence of the trouble.

But not all of these points are to be considered disadvantageous. On the contrary, their very flexibility is an advantage over the myopic and senile bureaucracy of the large enterprise, so bound by regulations as to be incapable of acting except by the book. If smaller enterprise's management takes a correct decision it can be immediately put into practice and if trial shows the idea to be inadvisable it can be instantly dropped. This mobility is something which is out of the question for a large enterprise which moves in deliberate organized steps.

Now comes the problem of defining the smaller enterprise from the QC standpoint. I wish to offer the following yardstick. *"It is an enterprise which cannot maintain specialists in QC techniques on its staff."* Or we may say that QC-wise, a smaller enterprise is one that cannot maintain a section or department specifically charged with QC activities.

A large enterprise can afford to maintain experts with a mastery of experimental, planning, and other advanced QC techniques, and they also have young university graduates who can be given this type of training. It is also possible for them to establish a Quality Control or Quality Assurance Section to handle the paperwork involved in encouraging QC activities throughout the organization.

In contrast, the majority of Japan's smaller enterprises, faced with a serious shortage of technically trained people, find it difficult to assign even high-school-trained technicians, let alone university graduates, to the single field of quality control. One still finds numerous cases of smaller enterprises who, forced by their parent company to adopt QC, have simply hung a sign reading 'Quality Control' on the old Inspection Section. The parent company is satisfied but the inner workings remain the same, and there is no resemblance to the true company-wide QC programme.

It must be understood that the QC Circle offers the best method by which such smaller firms can further their quality control activities and renovate their structure. It is this type of practical activity, centred on the foremen, which offers the best and quickest route to qualitative improvements in the shop.

Japan is rapidly losing its traditional attractiveness as a place of cheap high-quality labor. Large enterprises, in search of labor, are branching out into the countryside with factories employing hundreds and carrying out further expansion. But recently the supply of young workers has fallen behind the demand even in the provincial cities, making it necessary to build women's dormitories and recruit junior and senior high school graduate girls from the deep country. In five years Japan will be faced with the same necessity as America and West Germany — of employing foreign workers who cannot speak the language.

For this reason, first-echelon supervisors must be trained to give them the leadership capability required to cope with these changing conditions.

SMALLER ENTERPRISES AND QC CIRCLE ACTIVITIES

The QC Circle and enterprise activities

QC Circles, at bottom, differ markedly in one way from the sports, hobby, and other circles so often encountered in companies. That is, that results cannot be achieved without an overt joining of hands with executive level personnel.

The raising of the level of quality in the shop has always sprung from education, effected by the daily improvement of shop work. The content of the concrete problems taken up and the programmes for improvement cannot progress even a step without executive cooperation. Indeed, the achievement of any result would be impossible.

The QC Circle is more than just a set of attitudes. It is a movement which is made into a habit through actual practice. Small enterprise managers should see for themselves the examples which have succeeded in so many other enterprises so that they may obtain a clear understanding of the QC Circle. This understanding of the QC Circle will be gained faster by executives listening to reports from foremen and QC Circle members from various industries as given in nationwide QC Circle conferences and by executives pondering how best to apply them to their own enterprise, rather than by theoretical analysis.

QC Circles are peculiar to Japan. Here, the personnel in general are inculcated in application of QC techniques to the design, development, production, subcontracting and all other phases of management with the result that the companies no longer need QC specialists as in America. In Japan, there is little practice of concepts like Taylor's theory of division of labor, that the worker is simply to follow the drawings and specifications prepared by an engineer. Here, the work force takes the responsibility for quality while QC specialists simply spot-check and handle the paper work involved in spreading implementation of quality control.

This approach leads inevitably to the training of foremen in QC. The foreman in a Japanese factory differs basically from his American counterpart. There are many enterprises in which his position as 'working boss, leader, and teacher' is fully accepted by the work force. As a result, the number of people in Japan who have undergone QC training reaches a high level — unimaginable in the U.S. — and the trained personnel are more widely spread over all levels of management. That is the opinion of Dr Juran who goes on to say the following on the relationship between the circles and management:

"The most astonishing aspect of the QC Circles has nothing to do with quality control. What is astonishing is the degree to which the Japanese have succeeded in harnessing the energy, ingenuity and enthusiasm of the work force to the unsolved problems of the company." (See his article, "The QC Circle Phenomenon," in *Industrial Quality Control,* January, 1967.)

He also remarks that Japan has left behind outdated Western theories (see page 16) Thus he holds that it is essential to trust the work force and further says: "All this is in refreshing contrast to the painted, noisy spectacles which characterize all too many of our (Western) motivational programmes. The speeches are made, the posters go up, the pledge cards are signed, the hot potato is thrown into the lap of the operations. Yet, except as a show for customer relations, what good is it if the basic assumptions are defective?"

Juran characterizes the QC Circle movement, which he believes is based on the concept that the confidence of the work force is the fundamental factor of management, as "a brilliant achievement — a *tour de force* in management leadership," and concludes his essay by saying, "Nowhere else have I seen industrial companies succeed in so constructively harnessing the interest, the time and the ingenuity of the work force to the myriads of intra-departmental problems — not only problems of control, but problems of breakthrough as well."

Now let's try replacing the 'Japan' in Dr Juran's analysis with 'Japan's smaller enterprises.' For it may well be that QC Circle activities are a type of revolutionary quality programme better suited to smaller enterprises than to large ones.

In particular, pressed by the trend of liberalization of trade, and by accelerating technological innovation, every country is faced with a serious shortage of technological personnel. This problem is particularly severe in Japan's smaller enterprises, and as yet no satisfactory means has been found for its solution. Even if it is possible to obtain the services of young employees fresh from colleges and universities of technology, ill-conceived or half-baked technological plans would proliferate, causing more and more trouble. However, through the use of the QC Circles, technical production problems which resisted conventional treatment under the guidance of design engineers, have yielded to solution. As a result, it has been possible to make up for the technological personnel shortage, particularly as it affects the smaller shop.

When it is considered that smaller enterprises find it difficult to plan for regular year-by-year attraction of technological talent, it will be seen that the thorough training of middle-aged or older foremen in QC techniques is the shortest road to quality improvement and solving the problem of a shortage of engineers. QC Circle activities must be inculcated not just as a set of techniques, and must be understood at the topmost echelons of smaller enterprises as the best means of altering the basic structure of such enterprises and eliminating the chronic gap between them and the big enterprises.

Correct development of the QC Circle

QC Circle activities involve a basic change in habits of thought and will not succeed through aggressive prodding alone. It is necessary to spend a great deal of time in repetition, modifying procedures first in one way, then in another, to achieve persuasion.

And the first step is for management to attain a correct understanding of the QC Circle. This means not just reading a few books, calling in a consultant or two and 'thinking it over,' but actually seeing, in person, the scope and method of activities.

As previously mentioned, though the QC Circle is an independent movement, if the solid backing of executives is missing, it will degenerate into just another hobby club and fail to contribute productive effort.

It also, then, is in this sense of preventing such an eventuality that the manager must have a correct understanding of the QC Circle and must stand ready in the background to offer cooperation. The more such everyday improvements are carried out aggressively by the circles, the more the circles should come to demand design change, method improvement, new jigs and tools, improvement of the voucher system and changes in work assignment. And the results of studying each everyday improvement must be put into effect even if it does involve more staff work and a little extra expenditure. Otherwise, the whole thing will end in a mere intellectual exercise.

While it may be said that the QC Circle movement, in the long view, is a revolution in our approach toward quality, it is not a spiritual movement. It is necessary that foremen and workers search out the problems that confront them day-to-day in their work. They should, through the QC Circles, take practical steps toward a concrete solution for each problem, as it occurs, in order to gradually gain self-confidence. That is to say, the QC Circle movement is something to be appreciated by the participants themselves through practice; not something to be understood merely through theory and lectures.

Although I realize how busy the management and executive personnel of these smaller enterprises must be, I cannot refrain from suggesting that they become QC Circle members and really pitch in themselves. There is no incongruity in presence in the QC Circles of section or department managers. Get together, find some of your own most pressing problems and use the Deming cycle of Plan, Do, Check and Act.

What are the aims of the QC Circle movement?

We often come across smaller enterprise managers who claim that "QC seems to involve too many statistical technicalities" or "Our company isn't ready for it." This view is mistaken in the extreme, and is primarily the result of ignorance as to the true aims of QC Circle activities.

The first aim is, so far from trying to fill the shop workers with various statistical techniques, rather to *raise the quality-consciousness of first echelon supervisors and ordinary workers* who, in the face of technological innovation, are striving day and night for better quality shops.

The second aim is *development of leadership in these first echelon supervisors.* Particularly in smaller enterprises there is a relatively large number of 'gladhanding' supervisors who, in the quick-paced technological change of the factory, are eventually left behind their subordinates to become straw bosses or mere caretakers. There are the people who can be re-educated in their circles to be trustworthy superiors and effective leaders.

The third aim is *attainment of the capacity for independent action.* The QC Circle, consisting of people doing the same job, is incomparably well suited to encouragement of attentiveness to work, discovery of immediate problems, study of them for improvement and bringing them to the controlled condition.

The fourth aim is *inculcation of live QC techniques.* As distinct from material learned in texts and lectures, analysis, consideration and improvement of problems occuring on the job demand that the worker be able to use the techniques as easily as his own hands and feet. And the more difficult techniques are not something that can be handled in smaller enterprises.

In the first place, both theoretical and economic considerations indicate that even the process of educating workers in some complex technique will involve a large number of drop-outs. The feeling will spread that QC costs more than it is worth and that it would be easier to just go on as before, trusting to experience and intuition.

The second is that even if a complex statistical technique were mastered, smaller enterprises who are pressured to put every available hand to work, could not possibly afford the time to perform all the calculations required.

There is the further danger that even where there are available one or two people who make a hobby of handling statistics, they will become less and less able to follow the complex and varied problems of the shop, and will simply drift to the sidelines.

The fifth aim is *building of a good human relationship*. The habit of getting together and thinking as a group and apportioning activities is very effective in improving human relations and a feeling of belonging. The necessity of *all personnel participating in a QC Circle* is evident in this point. Cooperation in coming to grips with a problem and working step by step for its solution is what makes for better human relations.

Development of the advantages of smaller enterprises

In smaller enterprises, there are obviously a number of disadvantages compared to large enterprises on the scale of operation, the number of people involved and the funds available. There are also many examples of QC activities which started as a result of coercion by the parent company.

On the other hand, however, may it not be said that in contrast to a large enterprise's QC officer who concentrates on training his circle to produce uniform and prettily constructed activity reports, a smaller enterprise may have a programme at once more realistic and more fruitful. This is due to the following reasons.

Since the organization is small, management decision, once taken, can be put into immediate practice. Thus, it is possible to take appropriate action whenever the situation changes enough to warrant it. It is also easier to tell when a procedure becomes too mechanical to stimulate interest, or when it is mistaken in direction.

The manager of an enterprise where QC Circle activity is conducted can obtain its immediate benefit, i.e. suitable evaluation can be carried out. Also, in a smaller enterprise with a few circle members, meetings to announce results can be held more frequently. All the members thus receive a continued stream of fresh stimuli, and have many chances to think over and take pride in their methods.

In a certain printing company, the activity of the QC Circle members resulted in the step-by-step reduction of chronic product defects. The company president, after working with the members and effecting great savings, became the company's most enthusiastic advocate of the circle activity.

Whenever one of his young employees makes a report at a QC conference in some other region, the president invites his mother to go along and listen to him. One can but envy such mutual trust, where employer and employee work together. The 'Supervision through Trust' so often spoken of by Professor Eisaburo Nishibori shows the same line of thinking.

What are the points of superiority possessed by smaller enterprises? What are the particular characteristics of one's own company? These are the questions which must be fully considered in setting about development of a QC Circle.

Cases

Case 1

Eliminating machining errors
Masui Tanaka and Isao Takano*

We developed a rationalization movement covering our entire company, from April, 1965 to March, 1967 (the goal: annual savings of an estimated 50 million yen — US$140,000 in costs). The movement aimed mainly at reduction of costs, with the emphasis placed on improvement of the administrative structure through elimination of waste, overwork, and uneven work, and succeeded in saving an amount equal to 80 per cent of the goal.

In order to further guarantee the quality of our products, we adopted the slogan, 'Accurate Work from the Very Start.' Our Zero Defect movement was initiated in May, 1966 with the sub-sections organized as the unit groups for the movement; special priority was given to reduction of defective work (for cost reduction).

Through this movement the ratio of defective work was lowered by approximately 25 per cent during the two-year period from May, 1966 to March, 1968 proving that the movement was actually effective. Further, aiming at promotion of concrete measures for cost reduction and development of human capabilities (self-improvement), the ZD groups were decreased starting in February, 1968, in favour of QC Circle which totalled 113. The QC Circle movement of the company is conducted through educational activities, so that all shop problems can be solved independently by first-line personnel.

Organization of the QC movement

The QC Circle movement must have a close relation with on-the-line personnel. It is not necessary to elaborate how this relationship greatly affects the movement's achievements.

---

* Masui Tanaka is Subsection Chief of the Quality Control Section, and Isao Takano works in the Quality Control Section, Nagano Nippon Musen Kaisha, Nagano City.

QUALITY CONTROL CIRCLE CASE STUDIES

Figure 1 Organization chart for achievement of goals

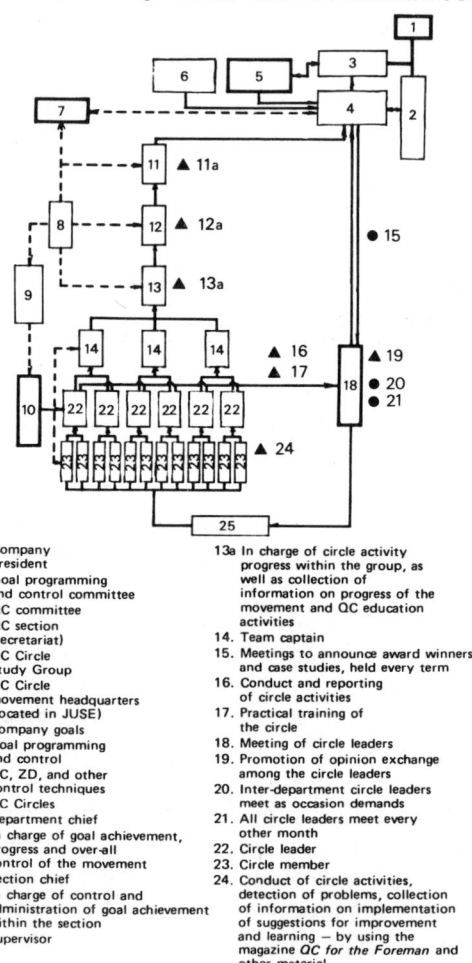

1. Company president
2. Goal programming and control committee
3. QC committee
4. QC section (secretariat)
5. QC Circle Study Group
6. QC Circle movement headquarters (located in JUSE)
7. Company goals
8. Goal programming and control
9. QC, ZD, and other control techniques
10. QC Circles
11. Department chief
11a. In charge of goal achievement, progress and over-all control of the movement
12. Section chief
12a. In charge of control and administration of goal achievement within the section
13. Supervisor
13a. In charge of circle activity progress within the group, as well as collection of information on progress of the movement and QC education activities
14. Team captain
15. Meetings to announce award winners and case studies, held every term
16. Conduct and reporting of circle activities
17. Practical training of the circle
18. Meeting of circle leaders
19. Promotion of opinion exchange among the circle leaders
20. Inter-department circle leaders meet as occasion demands
21. All circle leaders meet every other month
22. Circle leader
23. Circle member
24. Conduct of circle activities, detection of problems, collection of information on implementation of suggestions for improvement and learning — by using the magazine *QC for the Foreman* and other material
25. QC Circle activities

Our company emphasizes this point, and it conducts the movement through the company structure so that it may develop and become more effective. The organization of the movement is shown in figure 1.

Formation of a QC Circle

A QC Circle consists of about 10 people who do similar types of work which may come under the same job category. Its leader is chosen, as a rule, by the circle itself.

Meetings of QC Circle leaders
The QC Circle leaders meet regularly every other month to discuss circle activities and study problems of circle operations in order to promote inter-circle communication, to strive for mutual enlightenment, to co-ordinate inter-circle relations, and to enable each circle to conduct activities more effectively.

Circle study group
A Circle Study Group takes up matters related to operational improvement and provides guidance and education for the circles. It membership is open to supervisory personnel.

Linkage with the departmental (or organizational) goal
The goal of each circle is always established independently. In order to link it with the goal of the department to which the circle belongs (or the organizational goal), it is incumbent on the circle to obtain the approval of its goal from the supervisor. Thus, the supervisors become aware of the circle movement, and its linkage with them is established.

Promotion of suggestions
All suggestions for improvement of the circle movement and any other department should be submitted using the 'Suggestion Form for Improvement.'

Progress and achievements of the QC Circle movement
Interim and final reports on the progress and achievements of the QC Circle movement are presented regularly. When necessary, reports may be requested at any time to show the status and results of the movement.

Appraisal of achievements and the award system
The company's Award System is applicable to the achievements of the QC Circles and their suggestions. Achievements independently declared by each circle are appraised on points including the degree of achievement, contribution and difficulty, and rated in classes A or B for awarding purposes.

Case study: Elimination of processing mistakes
Following is a case study of the achievements of the Lathe QC Circle, which has 10 members. This circle consists of personnel in

QUALITY CONTROL CIRCLE CASE STUDIES

charge of machining such basic parts as castings and machine parts, using milling and shaping machines.

Analysis of the status quo

In order to detect problems, the status quo was expressed as three Pareto diagrams, of type of errors, day of the week errors occurred, and time of the day errors occurred, which revealed:

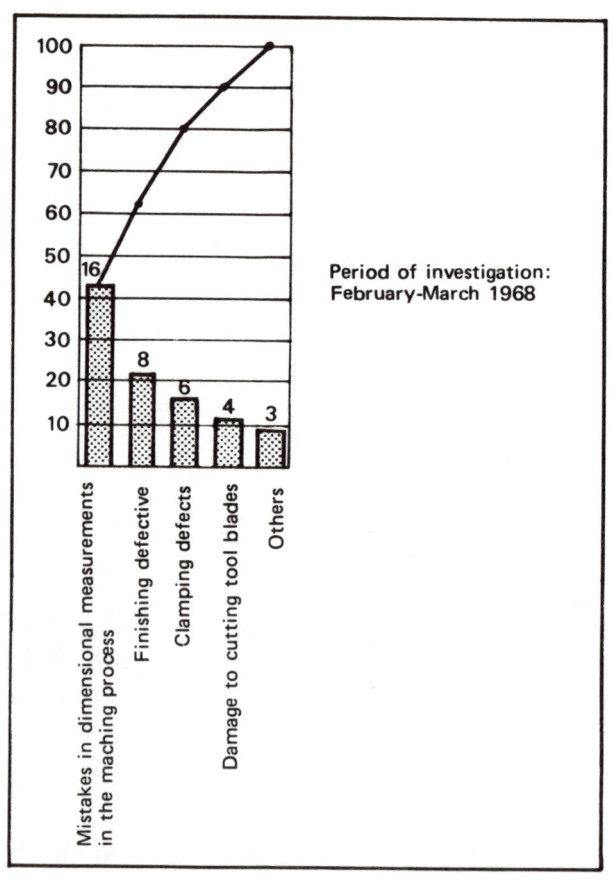

Figure 2 Pareto diagram for machining mistakes
(What machining mistakes occur most frequently)

Period of investigation: February-March 1968

ELIMINATING MACHINING ERRORS

a In regard to errors, there were mistakes in measuring machining dimensions and defects in finished work.
b Errors were concentrated on Mondays and Saturdays.
c Errors occurred most frequently at 8.50 to 10.00 a.m. and 1.00 to 3.00 p.m., when work was started and resumed.

Concerning erroneous dimensional measurements in particular, the goal was set at a reduction, of 50 per cent by the end of August (see figures 2, 3 and 4).

Figure 3 Frequency of mistakes according to day of the week

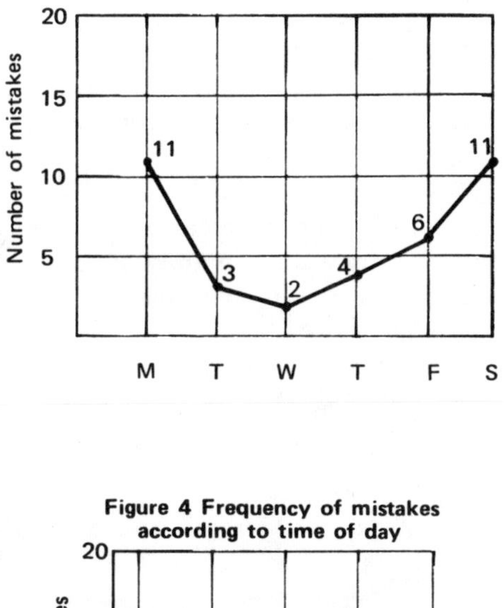

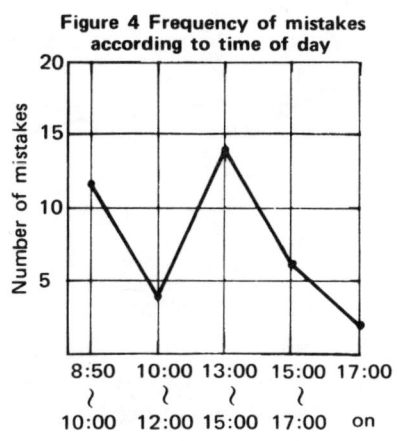

Figure 4 Frequency of mistakes according to time of day

Study of solutions to the problems

In solving the problems, a cause-and-effect diagram was prepared by all circle members, and as a result of studying it, it was found that the main causes were the omission of confirmation of pre- and post-operation checking and the lack of concentration at work.

Solutions to the problems

Pre-work meetings: In order to make the operators confirm readiness for work, pre-work meetings were held for three to five minutes.

Team inspection: Each operator was made to choose a partner (to form a team) and conduct team inspection on an alternating basis. This is significant in that each worker is made responsible for his own work.

A defective article, once detected, was not immediately re-processed but, in each case, the defect cause was studied, and in special cases, explanations and guidance were given to the circle members.

Results

Besides the reduction of errors in measuring by 50 per cent set as the goal, the reduction by approximately 40 per cent in all defective work has among the results achieved. The results are shown in figure 5.

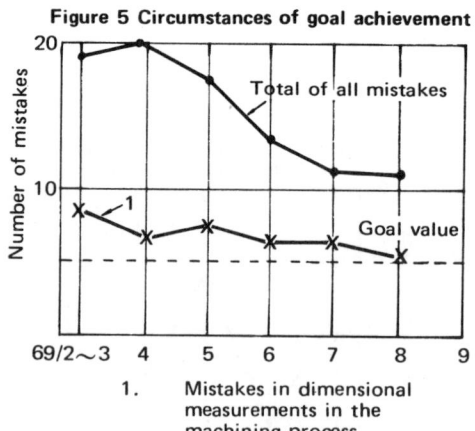

Figure 5 Circumstances of goal achievement

1. Mistakes in dimensional measurements in the machining process

Pre-work meetings resulted in early attendance at work and early return to work after the lunch hour. In addition, there were such indirect results as the maintenance of shop discipline and the improvement of quality consciousness.

Future themes

We assume the fact that a desire to solve problems independently on the line level has shown itself in various aspects is proof that our QC Circle movement, which developed from our ZD campaign, has begun to be absorbed and digested into the industrial texture of our company. It is observed in the departments, indirectly concerned with production, however, that the movement is somewhat stagnant, and we feel that a step forward must be made to conduct the movement on the level of the company as a whole. In the firm belief that to promote the movement in the departments indirectly concerned with production and make it well established in the company is the road leading to prosperity, we want to devote ourselves to bringing the movement to a company-wide level.

Case 2

Reduction of dimensional defects in felt
Hideo Saeki[*]

The Ichikawa Woolen Textile Co. manufactures felt for dewatering in papermaking, pulp making, and other industrial purposes. Electro-bonded textiles are also made.

The QC Circle movement was formally initiated in November, 1966. Before this, the senior staff members held informal meetings with their assistants to discuss improvement of the manufacturing processes. Although these meetings promoted mutual understanding, results were limited and therefore the QC Circle movement was introduced.

QC had already been introduced in the company and because extensive training had been given to the foremen, the movement made a good start. In less than two years after its start, seven reports on the movement's achievements were made public and some were even announced by younger employees. The movement is highly effective in correcting chronic defects in processes. Three examples of improvement are introduced below.

Reduction of dimensional defects in felt for papermaking

Felt for use in papermaking is manufactured in endless belt form and must meet strict specifications. The finishing section is responsible for maintaining the specified dimensions and it was in this section that the goal to reduce the dimensional defects was first established. The QC Circle movement was organized by the fulling (shrinkage) machine group.

---

[*] Hideo Saeki is Senior staff member, Control Section, Production Department, Ichikawa Woolen Textile Co., Ichikawa City, Chiba Prefecture.

Analysis of the status quo
A cause-and-effect diagram was prepared, the main cause for defects were sought and data on them were stratified by individual workers, specific machines and different product lines. Data recording was continued over the one-year period from March, 1966, and the Pareto analysis then prepared showed that the problem was caused by certain workers.

Results of the analysis
The investigation of errors in measurement of lengths of felt by the workers revealed·that only a slight deviation was found in the work done by older workers (over seven years of service) and that the problem lay mainly with the junior (three to six years) and new workers (less than two years).

Measures taken for solving the problem
1 Senior workers were made to inspect the work of junior and new workers step by step. Defects were pointed out, and explanatory guidance was provided using data on the tendencies for over- or under-measurement.
2 Every week the standards to be maintained for the work were written on a blackboard to have the workers better understand them.
3 Utilizing the all-workers assemblies held at the start and end of each day, the importance of teamwork was stressed for the benefit of all.
4 The checking responsibility of the skilled workers, acting for the senior staff members, was made clear, and the latter undertook inspection and gave guidance on the actual checking situation.

As many opportunities as possible were provided for improving understanding of the goals of the QC Circles and increasing the circles' freedom of action.

Achievements and future policy
Figure 1 shows that the dimensional defects decreased as successive measures were taken. In the future, since it is difficult to expect more achievements as long as the measures are taken by the 'one-circle-for-one-process' principle, it has been decided to have each circle cooperate with the two circles concerned with the preceding and following processes.

Table 1 Results of measures taken for solution of problems

Problems	Points checked	Action taken	Results
Length of base material per bolt	1. Correlation between the length of base material received and the length of final product 2. Variation between the dimensions measured by subcontractors and the standard dimensions for acceptance	Dimensional changes in the materials delivered by subcontractors	Complete elimination of short materials received
Base material dimensions	1. Checking of acceptance inspection of the materials received 2. Process checking and product inspection	1. Advice given to subcontractors about preventing defects 2. Standards established for handling below-standard base materials 3. Standards established for assorting materials for specific products	1. Reduction of defective materials 2. Simplification of work

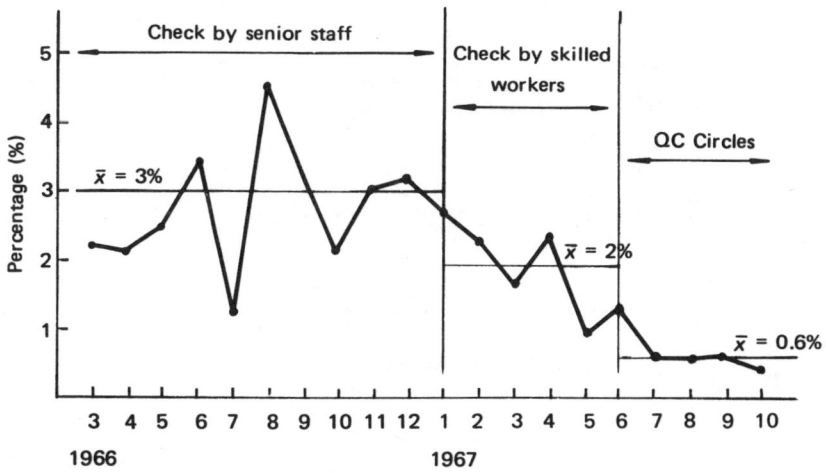

Figure 1 Changes in percent defective caused by wool fulling

QUALITY CONTROL CIRCLE CASE STUDIES

Countermeasures to reduce parallel unevenness in spinning slivers (Intermediate product)

The major problem in manufacturing felt to make belts for paper-making use is maintaining the specified thickness of the thread. Variation in thread thickness results in unevenness when felt slivers (an intermediate product) are made into a two-metre wide sheet. The goal of this programme was made the reduction in the occurrence of this unevenness. A QC Circle was formed by the fibre squad of the spinning section. The results of this circle's programme are introduced below.

Analysis of the causal factors

The main causal factors were identified at the first circle meeting and a cause-and-effect diagram was constructed (figure 3). Among the causes, as the mechanical one which was considered to exert the greatest influences, special attention was directed toward dirty and damaged fancy rollers. Before the QC Circle was formed, some of the dirt was removed when the needles were cleaned since it was felt that material stuck to the needle would impair its function. Thus, a test was carried out to compare the results before and after cleaning the roll.

The test was repeated five times on each machine. (For results, see figure 2). It is evident from this figure that the defective percentage was decreased one per cent by cleaning and if the number

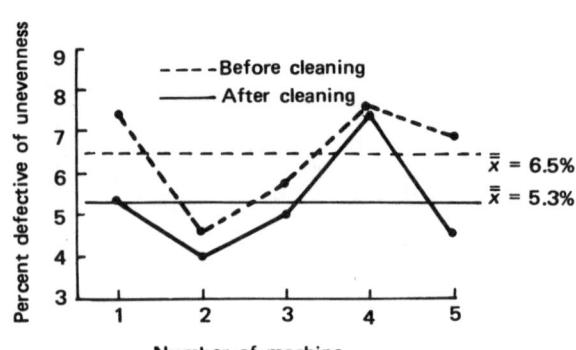

Figure 2 Comparison of percent defective before and after cleaning the fancy roll

Figure 3 Cause-and-effect diagram for parallel unevenness in slivers

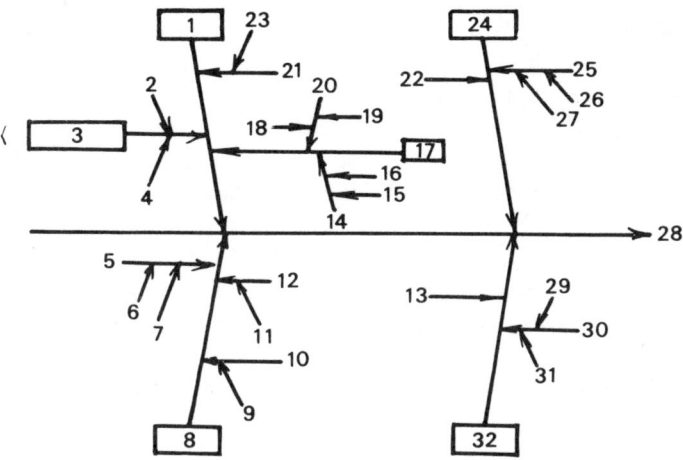

1.	Loom	17.	'C' stack
2.	Abnormality in head roller gauge	18.	Web felting squad
3.	Condenser	19.	Web width squad
4.	Abnormality in tape	20.	Abnormality in conveyor
5.	Individual differences in adjustment	21.	Weighing
6.	Differences in technical thinking	22.	Unsuitable materials
7.	Differences in ability to concentrate	23.	Weighing squad
8.	Workers	24.	Materials
9.	Inadequate standards	25.	Oil and water supply squad
10.	Inadequate adjustment	26.	Mixing by oil supply squad
11.	Insufficient training	27.	Drying squad
12.	Operation specifications not maintained	28.	Parallel unevenness in slivers
13.	Temperature and humidity fluctuation	29.	Measurement errors
14.	Impairment of needle functioning	30.	Inspection errors
15.	Inappropriate gauge	31.	Sampling errors
16.	Delay in cleaning needles	32.	Others

of damaged points on the fancy roller was considerable, it was replaced or repaired. The frequency of cleaning was increased, taking care that doing so had no adverse influence on the processing. These measures were added to the operation standards.

The next problem concerned the head roller gauges, used to maintain a constant opening between upper and lower rollers of carding machines. It was felt that if the gauge used was inappropriate, parallel unevenness was likely to occur. In order to determine the most appropriate gauge, the differences in percent defective were checked using 0.03-inch and 0.05-inch gauges, as shown in figure 4. This check revealed that the 0.03-inch gauge was better and this was then made the standard gauge. The group leader in the first shift now inspects the gauge each morning for abnormalities before starting work.

Cause-and-effect analysis was then made of the deviation in width of the web and we have reached a stage where action could be taken. No other factors are statistically significant.

Effectiveness

The percent defective of parallel unevenness before and after the QC Circle movement was introduced into our company is shown

Figure 4 Percent defective in relation to the belt roll gauge

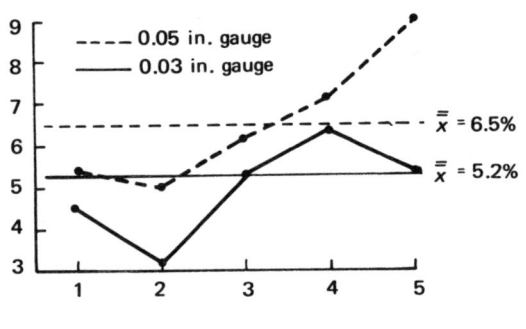

Number of machine

Figure 5 Changes in percent defective due to unevenness of slivers

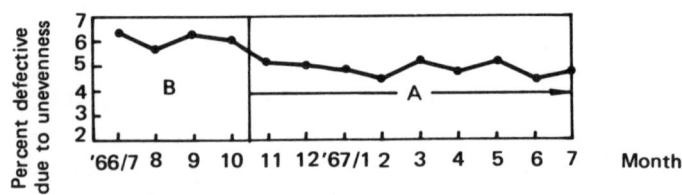

A   Progress of the QC Circle movement — average fraction defective was reduced to 4.8%.

B   Average percent defective before the circle movement began: 6.1%.

in figure 5. After its start, the average percent defective dropped from 6.1 per cent to 4.8 per cent and at this writing, it has reached a new low of 3.5 per cent as a result of thorough process standardization.

A decrease in the parallel unevenness fraction defective bears on reduction of the thread count fraction defective. The thread count fraction defective is shown in figure 6, from which it is evident that our effort to reduce it has been quite effective. In order to make further improvement, it is not only necessary to reduce the parallel unevenness of threads but also to improve the count inspection method. Efforts must be made to detect defects at an early stage and prevent potential defects.

Countermeasures to reduce defects in the base textile for electrodeposition

The electrodeposition process is as shown in figure 7. Nylon fibres are electrodeposited onto the base textile which is coated with a strong adhesive agent. This electrodeposited textile is used to make carpets, footwear, and furniture. In the electrodeposition section a QC Circle was formed to improve the yield percentage. The circle tackled the problem of defects in the case textile, which affected the yield percentage.

Outline of the electrodeposition process

The base textile after receipt from another company goes through a sequence of processes in this order: flossing, drying, and finishing.

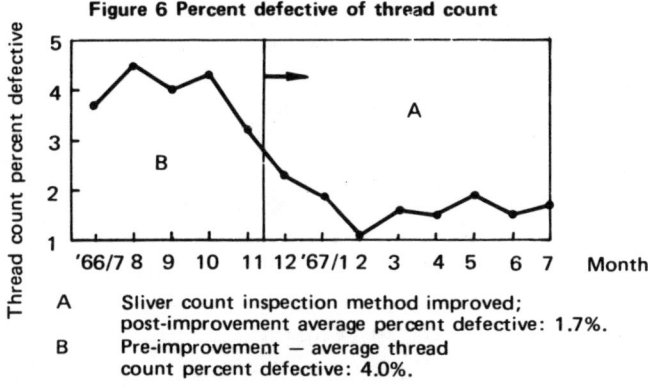

Figure 6 Percent defective of thread count

A Sliver count inspection method improved; post-improvement average percent defective: 1.7%.
B Pre-improvement — average thread count percent defective: 4.0%.

Figure 7 Electrobonding process

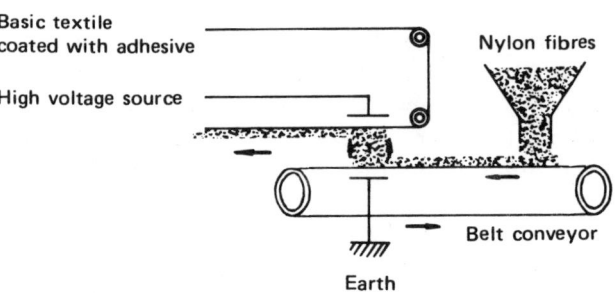

Analysis and countermeasures
There was a problem in the length of the base textile. The standard length of one bolt of the base cloth as purchased should be 120m plus 1m = 121m. It was noted, however, that from the latter half of August, 1967 some materials received were short of the standard length. Since the available percentage of the produce then decreased, the chiefs of the inspection and finishing departments carried out a correlative analysis in order to discover the cause of the problem. As can be seen in figure 8, the results showed a high degree of correlation ($\Upsilon = 0.9$m; yield percentage = 91 per cent). It was evident that the cloth became 0.8m longer in the finishing stage than in the inspection stage. When the lengths as received were insufficient, there was a discrepancy of 0.7m between the dimensions specified to the supplier and the dimensions as delivered. When this was rectified, the yield percentage of the base material returned to normal as shown in figure 9.

A means to reduce the base material defects was devised. Since base material defects have a great influence on the yield percentage of the product, the specifications for acceptance inspection were made stricter than the export specifications. The fraction defective average was 1.5 per cent and when the defects were found, the supplier was notified of them and discussions were held in which three points — causes of the defects, action, and action checking — were stressed. As shown in figure 10, the fraction defective began to drop at the end of August. From the results of process and product inspection, data concerning defects in the base materials were tabulated and intimated to the supplier.

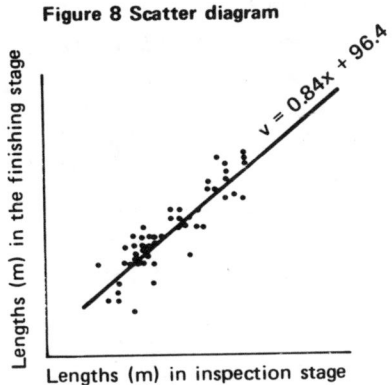

Figure 8 Scatter diagram

$y = 0.84x + 96.4$

Lengths (m) in the finishing stage

Lengths (m) in inspection stage

Figure 9 Yield percentage of the base material

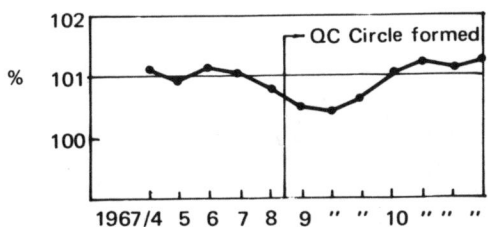

Figure 10 Frequency distribution table of percent defective

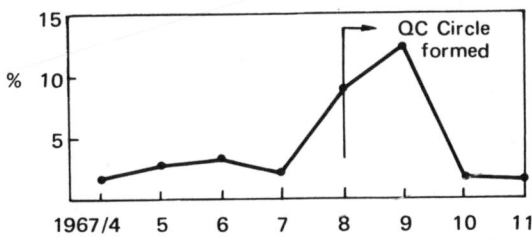

In order to reduce the number of processing steps, tolerance limits for felt which did not meet standard requirements were established, and the standards for handling and sorting such felt by specific uses were prepared.

Results

Results of this programme are listed in table 1. In the future, standards will similarly be established for all types of base materials on the basis of past experience and these results, and efforts will be made to improve yield percentages. Finally, problems arising from external suppliers will be tackled by conducting strict checks within our company, and we are confident that furthering the spirit of cooperation between the company and its subcontractors is a prerequisite for solving these problems.

Case 3

Rewind cutting process improved

Yasuo Kumon*

This case study's locale is the Kinki Region where the QC Circle activity of such companies as Matsushita Electric has attracted considerable attention.

On hearing, in 1964, of participation in QC Circle conferences by QC Circles of companies in the Kinki Region and Osaka, we became quite interested. In the following year, the post of quality control superviser was elevated to the level of an office and QC Circle activity was begun as a result of extensive effort on the part of the many individuals at this plant. (At present, about 100 persons from our plant participate in general QC Circle meetings in the Kinki Region and Osaka.)

At the time of QC Circle formation, there were many doubts and problems but these were resolved in due time by discussions. With deepening of understanding, the movement has steadily progressed to its present state.

Our QC Circle movement

At present, QC Circle activity is found in nearly all work areas of this plant. The number of QC Circles has steadily increased and totalled 30 in autumn, 1968. In departments working three shifts, QC Circle activity is divided according to area of responsibility and shift. The work of individual circles is carried out under the supervision of respective leaders and subleaders.

All circle activities are not at the same level because of differences in the circles' origins, but circle activity in all cases is progressing in step with the nature of work in individual areas. A broad classification of the work of these circles reveals the following three categories.

---

* Yasuo Kumon is in charge of quality control and technical investigation, Yodogawa Plant, Honshu Paper Manufacturing Co., Osaka.

1 Activities centred around study group meetings which serve to broaden knowledge.

2 Activity pertaining to personal problems and their relation to work, such as safety, regulations and human relations.

3 Activity relating directly to work, such as the factory manager's policies, efficiency improvement, revision of work, reduction of defects, and quality improvement.

Most QC Circles meet one or twice a month for one or two hours, outside of regular working hours. Depending on circumstances, there are times when objectives can be fulfilled during regular working hours.

To obtain close liaison among the various QC Circles and the office, meetings attended by the leaders are held twice a month, and leader training meetings are held periodically to provide leader education and training.

The results have been gratifying, with the movement gaining momentum in respect of numerous plans for improvement of work and quality, and of reports on experiences encountered as well as regular meetings for announcement of research results and QC Circle meetings outside the company.

To give the QC Circle a greater role, the subject of QC Circle improvement was taken up at the regular monthly quality control meeting in November in 1966 and 1967. As a result, opportunities were created to attend lectures and panel discussions outside the company, to have contact with QC Circles of other companies, to receive education, and to study by direct observation of plant functions. More recently, basic data covering 'QC Circle accomplishments at the Yodogawa Plant' has been compiled, leading to progress in QC Circle thinking and deepening the understanding of quality. The QC organization is illustrated in figure 1.

As discussed in meetings and panel discussions, it is necessary to have 100 per cent participation with everyone from the top down exhibiting true interest. The plant alone is insufficient, as there must be an atmosphere of human understanding among all employees including clerical workers to produce QC Circle organizational strength. Mutual development and spirit are vital. Development of the true QC Circle is in part the result of squarely facing the issues. The present trend is toward a movement in which everyone provides spirited contributions.

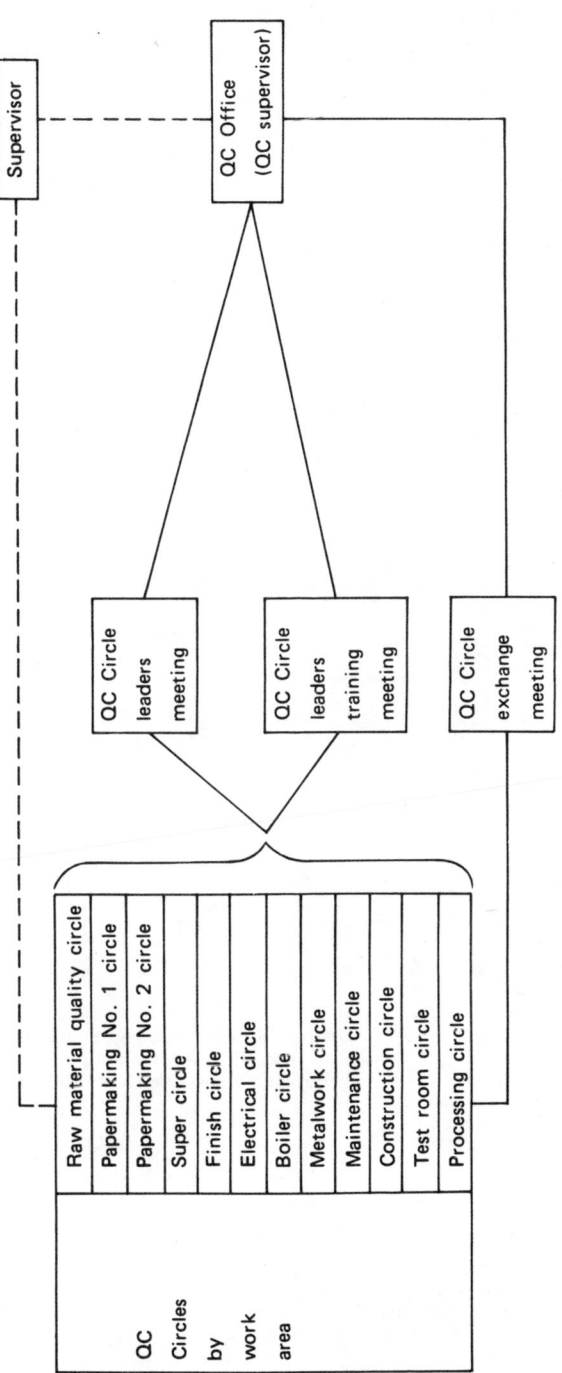

Figure 1 QC Circle organization at the Yodogawa Plant

QUALITY CONTROL CIRCLE CASE STUDIES

Case study: 'Finish' QC Circle (women)

We're responsible for final finishing work in the manufacture of paper. One of our processes is rewind cutting. We wish to describe problems pertaining to efficiency improvement as encountered by our QC Circle and to relate the results of our efforts in improving the process.

Description of process

There are two types of paper manufactured by our plant, roll and cut. For finishing, bobbin machines and winders are used for roll paper, while cutters are used for cut paper.

When it is necessary to cut paper into smaller dimensions, the paper is unrolled as necessary and cut with a guillotine cutter. After selection, finishing is made to the desired size. This is known as the rewind cutting process (see figure 2).

In the rewind cutting process, paper is cut by a series of cutting heads radially attached to a drum. The length of the cutting head

Figure 2 Old and new rewind processes

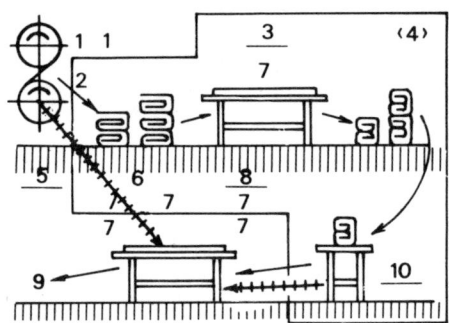

1. Male worker
2. Old process
3. Sorting
4. (Old process)
5. Rewinder
6. New process
7. Female worker
8. Unfolding work
9. Guillotine cutter
10. Table

Note: Solid arrows and enclosed portion of diagram represent the old process. Hatched arrows represent the new process.

Before-and-after comparison

Before improvement		After improvement	
1.	Independent operations	1.	Continuous operations
2.	Loss from stacking products	2.	Loss eliminated
3.	Fold rejects caused by stacking	3.	Fold rejects eliminated
4.	Two men and four women required	4.	Two men and two women required

Figure 3 Rewinder

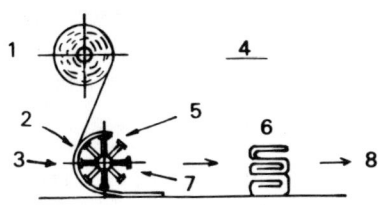

1. Roll
2. Unrolling
3. Length of cutting head spokes adjustable
4. Specified length rewound for cutting to required dimensions
5. Cutting heads
6. Three folds
7. Drum
8. Selection

spoke is adjustable; extension of the spokes increases the distance between cutting heads and it is by this means that the size of the paper which is cut is controlled. Paper is thus cut at fixed intervals at a fixed speed and then fed to the guillotine cutter for final trimming.

The process before improvement
Prior to incorporating modifications, rewinding was made and the process carried out as follows:
1. The roll to be used was positioned at the top of the rewinder and was unrolled and cut by passing the paper around a drum below.
2. Paper thus cut was folded three times and stacked for sorting.
3. The folded paper was picked up by the sorter, placed on a table, and spread out for sorting.
4. Sorted paper was folded four times and stacked.
5. The folded paper was unfolded to permit feeding to the guillotine cutter. The first step was placing the paper on a table in preparation, after which it was transferred to another table for actual unfolding. Three women handled the work.
6. The prepared paper was then fed to the guillotine cutter.

Reason for selecting this theme
The rewind cutting process had been carried out in the same manner for a long, long time. With such a complicated work flow, the number of workers was considerable and paper loss high. For these reasons, it seemed that there must be some better procedure and hence the subject was taken up at QC Circle meetings.

Investigation and corrective measures

Discussions were held with senior personnel and those men who actually handled rewinding. The first point to attract attention was work duplication. Therefore, we looked for a way to combine jobs.

The procedure had been established many years ago and naturally there was resistance to change. Through the medium of several discussions, understanding and cooperation were realized. After several trials, the process was modified as described below.

Process after modification
1 In order to eliminate some of the labor involved in sorting, sorting at the time of rewinding was eliminated. (This was possible because of low speeds involved.)
2 The rewound paper was directly spread out and transported to a sorting table, at which inspection-like sorting was carried out. In one operation, the paper was spread, sorted, and edges were aligned, after which the paper was fed to the guillotine cutter. Figure 2 presents a comparison of the process before and after modification.

Results and conclusion

As shown in the figure, the process has been greatly simplified. The paper loss has been reduced, quality improved, and efficiency raised. Only two women were required under the new procedure, enabling transfer of the others. By removing unnecessary fixtures, floor space was more effectively utilized. This enhanced safety and made the work easier.

In the future, we want to take up more problems in a positive manner and to contribute more to work improvement, production increase, and efficiency.

Credit for this case study belongs to Misses Kiyoe Okumi, Akiko Kiuchi, and Muneko Kokabu.

Case 4

Reduction of defects in metal plates

Michi Tanaka[*]

The Funabashi Factory of Nihon Kentetsu Co. has 2,700 employees and is an operation division producing components for electrical equipment, heat exchangers, door sash, etc.

The company's QC Circle movement was started in 1964 and continued for three years under that name. In November, 1967, the 'Z' movement (this company's abbreviation for the ZD movement) was introduced with the QC Circles as the main units.

As a case study, the plant's QC Circle movement is introduced.

From the QC circles to the "Z" movement

The QC Circle movement began in 1964 with a QC course (2 hours a day for 5 days) for all group chiefs (about 100 persons). This course was made up mainly of easy QC techniques which could be put to use in the shop. After the course, checks were made to see to what degree the group chiefs were utilizing the techniques they had learned.

As a result, it was found that only about half the shops utilized the techniques. The necessity of rectifying this became apparent. November, 1964 was designated as quality control month and foremen from other companies came to observe our factory. In this way we learned first-hand of the situation concerning the QC Circle movement in other companies.

Between 1964 and 1965, the QC Circles were formed. At this time, about 30 per cent of all employees attended the circle meetings but by 1967, 55 per cent were attending. In November, 1967, the 'Z' movement was introduced and employees began to attend its meetings.

The switch from the QC Circles to the 'Z' movement was made for the following reasons: (a) changes in the general situation (the QC Circles had become routine); (b) to activate the movement in the clerical departments; (c) to attain participation of all employees (including new and part-time workers, etc).

---

[*] Michi Tanaka is from the Quality Control Section, Electrical Products Department, Funabashi Factory, Nihon Kentetsu Co. Funabashi City, Chiba Prefecture.

The most important reason, however, was to found a movement based on achieving the managerial goals of the company.

QC Circle administration

In the QC Circle movement, all staff departments were involved in the movement and the manufacturing section chiefs in all departments served as advisors.

The circles were divided into small groups of four or five persons and activities were organized in connection with daily work. The QC Circle organization is shown in figure 1.

Aims of the QC Circle movement

When the QC Circle movement began, the first objective was to acquaint all employees with QC techniques. For this purpose, they were allowed to observe the practical application of QC techniques to all kinds of problems no matter how simple. The next goal was to make the movement more effective by the appropriate application of QC techniques, to gradually eliminate defects and increase operational efficiency. At this writing, the operational efficiency of most groups is improving and work loss is being reduced in accordance with the goal of making the movement economically effective.

QC Circle training

To promote the effectiveness of the QC Circle movement, day-by-day instruction and training is essential. This company conducts on-the-job and other programmes for QC Circle and supervisory personnel, as outlined in table 1.

Problems concerning the QC Circle movement

An investigation of problems which arose concerning the QC movement revealed that lack of time was the major complaint (see figure 2). At present investigations are being conducted to get to the root of this problem and make improvements.

Case study: Reduction of defects in metal plates*

In our shop, we process metal plates for refrigerated showcases. We chose 'reduction of metal plates defects,' which is very pertinent for our work, as our circle's theme. The objective was to reduce the 7 per cent defective by half.

At team meetings we drew up a schedule for achieving the goal. All members agreed to the schedule and worked out a plan of cooperation.

---

* (Electrical Parts Manufacturing Section, Refrigeration subsection, Kobayashi Team)

Figure 1 Organization of the QC Circle Movement

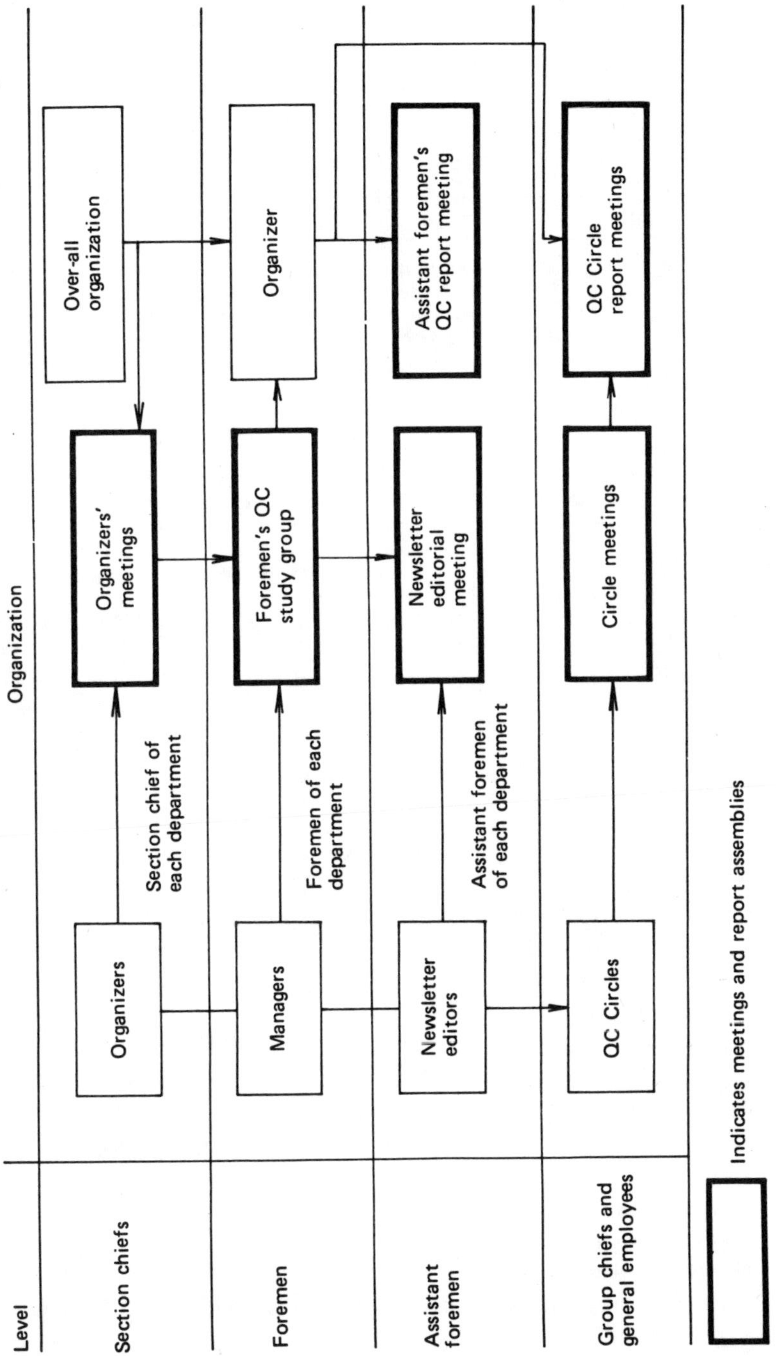

Level	Organization			
Section chiefs	Organizers	Section chief of each department	Organizers' meetings	Over-all organization
Foremen	Managers	Foremen of each department	Foremen's QC study group	Organizer
Assistant foremen	Newsletter editors	Assistant foremen of each department	Newsletter editorial meeting	Assistant foremen's QC report meeting
Group chiefs and general employees	QC Circles		Circle meetings	QC Circle report meetings

☐ Indicates meetings and report assemblies

QUALITY CONTROL CIRCLE CASE STUDIES

Table 1 Training for QC Circle and supervisory personnel

Level	Training
Foremen	Foremen's QC study groups (to meet monthly). Study of themes of common interest to foremen (Example: 'What are the essential duties of a foreman?').
Assistant foremen	Assistant foremen's QC study groups (to meet monthly). Themes given for individual study and progress reports given.
QC Circle — squad chiefs and general employees	1. Circle meeting for leaders or circle members (more than once a month). 2. Intra-company report meetings (monthly). 3. Intra-company distribution of the newsletter *QC for Everyone* 4. Circulation of the magazine *QC for the Foreman*.

(Although the name has now been changed to the 'Z' movement, training is essentially the same as in this table)

Inspection of general conditions
The first step was to clarify the general situation concerning metal defects and determine their causes. The conditions were investigated by means of a Pareto diagram (figure 3) and a cause-and-effect diagram (figure 4).

Countermeasures
At the team meetings, the following countermeasures were devised:
Changing finishing tools: In the finishing process of the welding section the paper foiling step was changed to buffing. As shown in figure 5, the paper foil is narrow and tends to damage the plates. By using a wide buffer, such damage is prevented and there is also a saving in tool costs.
Improvement in the method of stacking materials: After finishing, the plates were stacked on a wooden pallet. However, damages and scars occurred during transport and restacking, and therefore a

hand cart as shown in figure 6 was used instead of the pallet.
Control of spot welding: Checks made in the morning and afternoon on test pieces of equal thickness eliminated any defects due to changes in conditions.

Figure 2 Problems of the Circle Movement

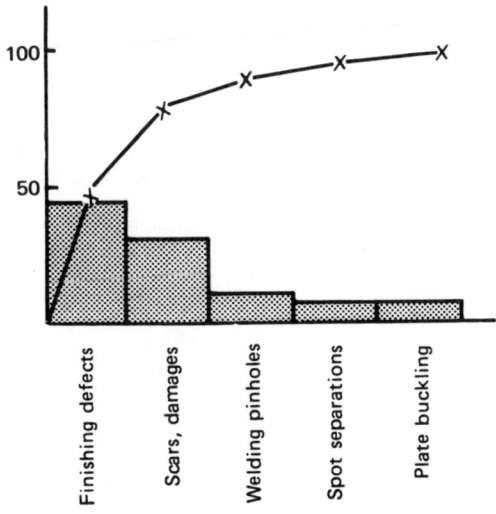

Figure 3 Pareto diagram for plate defects

QUALITY CONTROL CIRCLE CASE STUDIES

Figure 4 Cause-and-effect diagram for plate defects

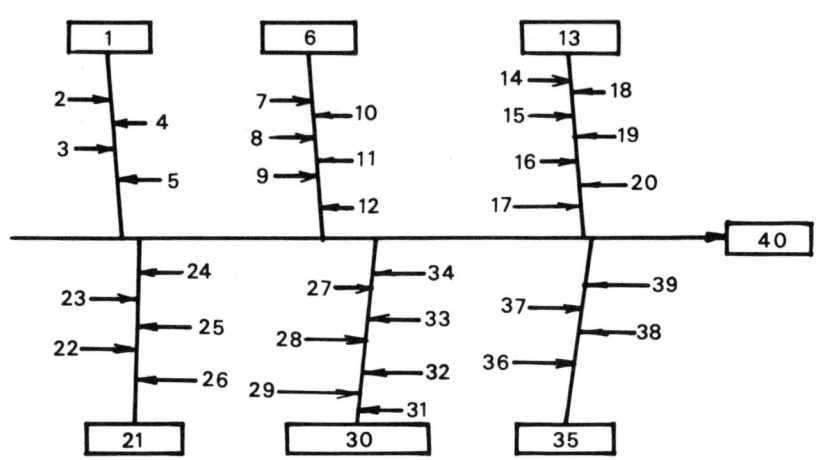

1.	Materials	21.	Control methods
2.	Damages	22.	Tool changing specifications
3.	Rust		
4.	Liquid for bending plates	23.	Feedback
		24.	Standardization
5.	Two-ply plates	25.	Checking of method applications
6.	Operation methods		
7.	Stacking	26.	Communication
8.	Transport	27.	Unexpected breakdowns and shutdowns
9.	Work location		
10.	Storing	28.	Obsolete equipment
11.	Arrangement of processing steps	29.	Operation
		30.	Equipment (welding)
12.	Work sequence	31.	Chippings
13.	Workers	32.	Cooling water
14.	Understanding the work	33.	Voltage variations
		34.	Checking of equipment
15.	Differences between individuals		
		35.	Finishing tools
16.	Differences in skills	36.	Sander
17.	Quality consciousness	37.	File
18.	Physical strength	38.	Buffer
19.	Condition of health	39.	Paper foil
		40.	Characteristics resulting in metal plate defects
20.	Volition		

Control of differences in worker skills: Experienced workers were paired with trainees in an effort to standardize work, especially the welding process.

Use of slogans: Each team decided on a slogan and everyone was urged to live up to the slogan. Slogans included 'Be Careful while Operating the Equipment,' 'Improve Attendance,' and 'Bear Responsibility for Your Own Work.'

Posting defect percentage control charts: The daily percentage of defects was posted in a place where it could be seen by everyone, and all workers were urged to be careful.

Results

As can be seen from figure 7, a combination of the above-mentioned countermeasures resulted in controlling the defects below the goal line or upper limit of defects. At present, the percentage of

Figure 5 Improvement in the finishing tool

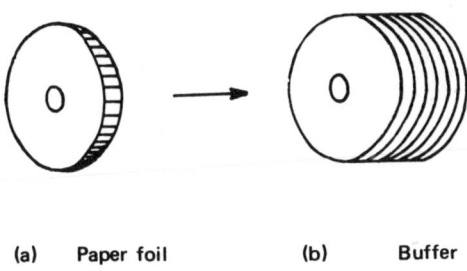

(a)   Paper foil   (b)   Buffer

Figure 6 Improvement in material handling

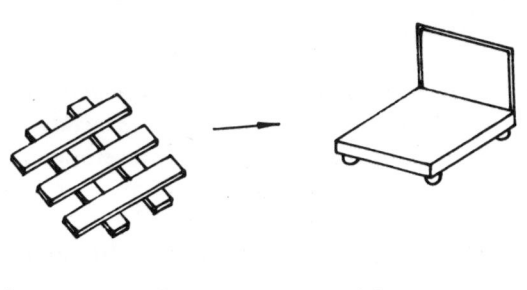

(a)   Wooden pallet   (b)   Hand cart

correcting defects is as low as one to two per cent and efforts are being made to lower it even more.

Considerations

What is especially evident about this team movement is that there is no royal road to reduce defects, and it is considered that what must be done is everyone should faithfully carry out the work assigned to him. It is also considered important to provide thorough initial training for inexperienced workers such as part-timers and day laborers in order to minimize the differences in skills.

The QC Circle and ZD movements are remarkably effective at the outset. The case study introduced here is a success story, but

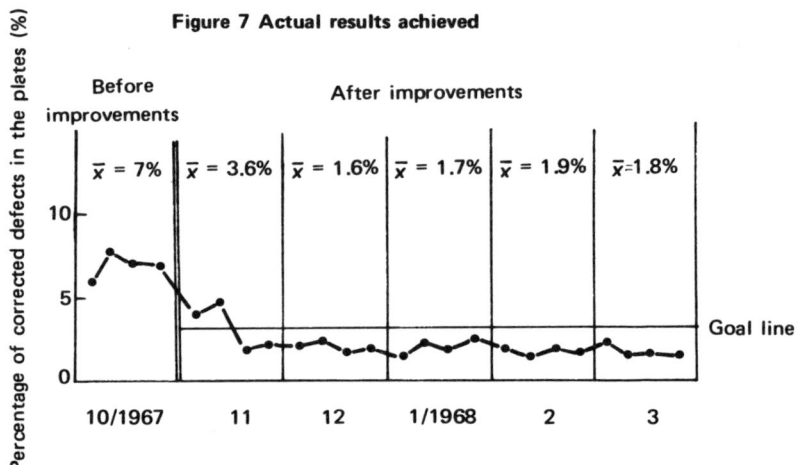

Figure 7 Actual results achieved

many teams are prone to run out of steam in the middle of their projects and for this reason the movements will not last long.

This is no doubt partly a problem of promotion, but from the above considerations it would seem that the morale of all personnel counts most.

Our present movement is too much concerned with clearing up defects and is therefore weak when it comes to production preparations or to looking ahead to prevent the development of defects.

Trouble, when the mass production of an article begins, will have to be eliminated by concerted efforts, in the model design and trial production stages, to standardize quality and make operations efficient.

Case 5

Reducing refrigerator component processing defects

Shigeo Tomizawa*

The Osaka factory of Toshiba manufactures electric refrigerators. After introduction of QC Circles to the plant, with the creation of four model circles in February, 1967, the number of circles and participants rapidly expanded. In late 1968 there were 100 circles. In the production departments, nearly all workers have joined circle activities.

Control and objectives of QC Circle activity

The basis of QC Circle activity is found in autonomous control by the members. The promotion of such control through the medium of suitable instruction and guidance from the organization is considered to be required for the growth of QC Circle activity. Major steps taken at the Osaka factory are described below.

1. QC Circle training and lateral support from group leaders and staff is furnished by a QC Circle advancement group consisting of a group leader and staff.
2. Meetings to announce current activities and recent results are held whenever necessary by the individual 'blocs,' while plant meetings are held twice a year. At the plant meetings, everyone is present, including the plant manager and the managing staff.
3. To keep interest in QC activities high, 'QC Circle News' is published once a month. This newsletter keeps all participants abreast of what other circles in the plant are doing and of what is discussed at general meetings at other factories.
4. Meaningful participation in meetings at other factories and making announcements of circles members experiences are highly valued. Many participate in general QC Circle meetings of the Kinki Branch of the QC Circle Headquarters.

---

* Shigeo Tomizawa is from the Osaka Factory, Tokyo Shibaura Electric Co., Ibaragi City, Osaka Prefecture.

QUALITY CONTROL CIRCLE CASE STUDIES

At the Osaka factory, QC Circles particularly encourage teamwork. Guidance is given in such a manner that persons other than the director may develop a feeling of leader-procedure which is vital in effecting growth from the bottom. The end result is a vast improvement in the work site atmosphere. From the standpoint of the plant, QC Circles are indispensable. To fulfill objectives, the following conditions apply.

1. Producing results by means of independent planning and action becomes a matter of developing an interest in maintaining company profit, that of a desire for increased production and of striving for improvement.
2. Through QC Circle activity, product quality must be maintained and improved, and improvements in productivity must be maintained. For this reason, the themes of circle activity are not to be sought in a narrow definition in terms of quality control, but should be related to all aspects of improvement of production. Engineers, as staff members, must be devoted to the development of manufacturing technology and to moving forward in the broad sense of the term.
3. Harmonious person-to-person relationships among workers and morale improvement are necessary.

Below are two case studies selected from those announced at factory meetings.

Case study: Measures for reducing dryer processing defects*
Establishing goals

A dryer is used to remove water from the freezing unit of refrigerators. The QC Circle for dryer assembly work set as its goal the solution of the following problems.

Most of the work of producing dryers was automated, meaning that even slight errors resulted in many defects.

The cost of copper material used was high, and associated loss considerable. This suggested that it was possible to reduce costs by eliminating production of defective items, i.e. by improving quality and stabilizing operations.

Due to these problems, the goal of 'reducing defective dryers' was established. The goal became a 40 per cent reduction of the total number of defects during the five months preceding the start of the project.

---

* Dryer QC Circle, nine members.

Status of activities

This QC Circle, in order to solve the problems outlined above, made full use of lunch periods and time after working hours. The following reveals the resultant development of the abilities of circle members and improvement in activities.

In connection with the development of the circle members' abilities, action was taken mainly on four points; viewing slides pertaining to circle activity case studies and the advancement of circle activity, establishing study groups to investigate dryer performance and operation, making work guidance slips showing work points and specifications, and in training of new workers.

Improvement in activities was attained mainly in three ways: the QC Circle made an exhibition panel depicting the production models, so that there would be no mistake concerning work on the various production models, and special attention was given to collecting and analyzing data, and understanding problems. In connection with the latter, the first step taken was to examine the nature of defects which had occurred in the preceding three months and making Pareto diagrams (figure 1).

As figure 1 reveals, cutting defects are responsible for 80 per cent of total rejects, and hence this problem was selected for examination. Cutting defects were then analyzed and another Pareto dia-

Figure 1 Pareto diagram showing the nature of defects

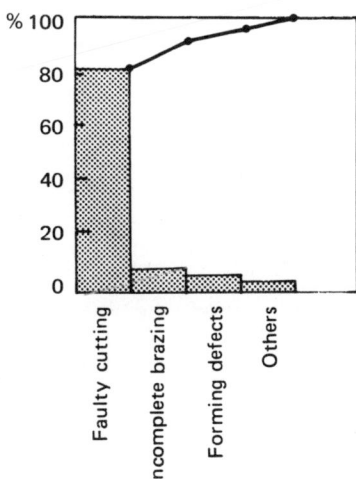

QUALITY CONTROL CIRCLE CASE STUDIES

Table 1 Problems and corrective measures

Problem		Corrective measure
1 Centre shift	1.	A new centre positioning pin was fitted to the jig for supporting the dryer centre, providing a stabilizing effect.
	2.	The number of outlets for supplying air to the centre positioning cylinder was increased from one to two, increasing the air pressure.
2 Faulty cutting	1.	Provision was made to periodically replace the bearings.
	2.	Rubber was used for feeding the pipe, preventing slippage.
3 Incomplete brazing	1.	A policy was adopted by which brazing material dropped to the floor was always cleaned before use.
	2.	A frame was fitted to the work bench, so that brazing material could not fall accidentally.
	3.	Faulty items were shown to those involved.
4 Faulty forming	1.	Construction of the dryer support jig used in the forming process was modified to permit correct forming.
	2.	The equipment was modified so that the dryer could not accidentally be inserted in the machine in the wrong direction.

gram drafted (figure 2). From this diagram, it is obvious that 50 per cent of cutting defects was due to centre shifting. Other problems were clearly shown.

Figure 2 Pareto diagram showing an analysis of faulty cutting

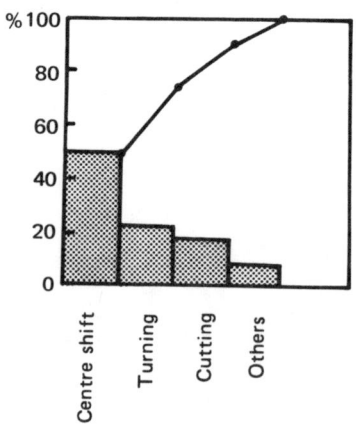

REDUCING REFRIGERATOR COMPONENT PROCESSING DEFECTS

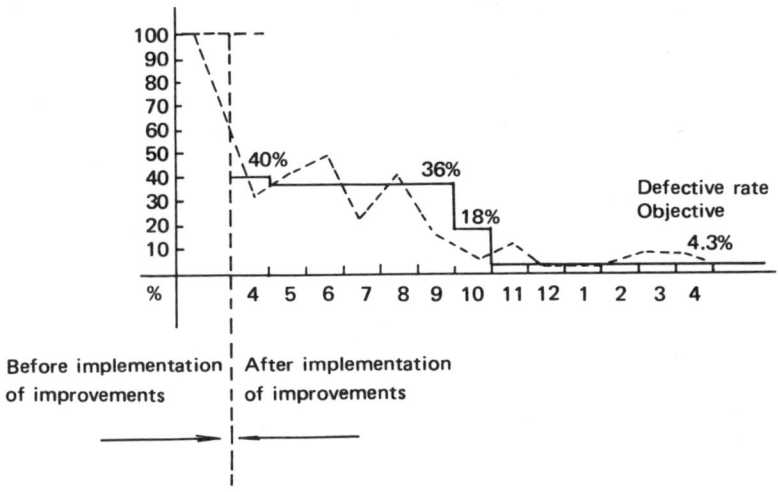

Figure 3 Rate of defectives

For determination of the source of trouble and corrective measures, a cause-and-effect diagram pertaining to cutting defects was prepared. The source of trouble in the case of other problems was checked and measures described in table 1 were taken.

Results
Through the development and corrective measures described above, the rate of defectives was drastically reduced as shown in figure 3 and table 2.
The saving realized as a result of reducing defectives amounted to 90,000 yen ($US250) per month.
From selection of the goal to the work itself, to confirmation of results, the will to work was outstanding because of the opportunity for all to do something with their own resources. Human relations vastly improved as a result of circle meetings.
The results were most gratifying.

Case study: Work improvement, improvement in efficiency and transport work
(Finish line N 4 QC Circle, 10 members)
Establishing the theme for action
In this work area, parts used in refrigerators are painted and transported to the assembly area. To improve production at this

point, the theme 'work improvement, improvement in efficiency and transport work' was adopted.

Activity status

As in the case of the QC Circle previously described, this circle also made the most of lunch periods and time after work. Discussions included problems pertaining to efficiency and quality in relation to present work methods; points requiring revision from the standpoint of improving work efficiency, and problems which would arise from incorporating revised methods.

Results

As a result of incorporating various corrective measures, 80,000 yen ($US222) a month was saved.

These two case studies represent only a portion of QC Circle activity at the Osaka factory. The activity of these circles is not only directed toward cultivation of a feeling for quality control but also toward instilling a desire to participate in positive improvement. In addition to improving personal relationships at work, there is also the aspect of an atmosphere of challenge. In brief, QC Circle activity contributes heavily to quality and produc-

Table 2 Before and after improvement

	Nature of modification	Before	After
1	Elimination of bolt rethreading (reduction of one person)	Paint adhering to the bolts of painted parts made threading of the nut impossible, necessitating recutting of threads.	As shown in this drawing, the indicated portion of the bolt was made thinner, making use of the nut possible without recutting threads.
2	Elimination of masking (reduction of three persons)	Masking of component portions not requiring paint was necessary.	By changing the method of supporting painted parts and altering the method of painting, the necessity of masking was eliminated.
3	Improvement of hooking parts on conveyor (reduction of one person)	As indicated in the sketch below, three parts (A, B and C) were hooked on the conveyor in the sequence shown Part A Part B Part C Workers A B C	The sequence of hooking parts on the conveyor was changed as shown in the sketch below. Parts previously hooked on the conveyor by Worker A were divided equally between the remaining two men, eliminating one person. Part B Part A Part C B C

WEIGHING OF RUBBER COMPOUNDING INGREDIENTS

		Man A: Part A, eight pieces in 36 seconds Man B: Part B, eight pieces in 55 seconds Man C: Part C, 10 pieces in 72 seconds	Man B: Part B, eight pieces } 86 seconds Part A, four pieces Man C: Part A, four pieces } 82 seconds Part C, 10 pieces
4	Improvement of conveyor work Improvement of hangers	Part A, four pieces Part B, four pieces { Part A, 16 pieces accomodated Part B, 8 pieces accomodated Part D, five pieces Part E, six pieces { Part D, 20 pieces Part E, 12 pieces	Part A, 7 pieces Part B, 8 pieces { Part A, 27 pieces Part B, 16 pieces Part D, five pieces Part E, six pieces Part D, 10 pieces { Part D, 30 pieces Part E, 12 pieces

By means of this modification, the number of pieces hooked was increased as shown in the following, and stock at the work site was reduced.

	Before modification	After modification
Number of pieces hooked (per day)	7,600 pieces	12,300 pieces (1.6 times)

Number of parts stocked at work site

Before modification | After modification
6000 — 5500
4000 — 4500
2000 — 900 400
Dec. Jan. Feb. Mar. April

101

tion improvements, and is vital in maintaining company profit at a desirable level.

In the 18 months since the inception of QC Circles at the factory, bee-like activity and tremendous results have appeared. Circle members are now striving to further improve the present status and to raise activity to higher levels. QC Circle efforts have put meaning into quality control at this plant.

Case 6

Simplification of the weighing of rubber compounding ingredients

Shunichi Harada[*]

Autonomous Circle movement

This company has always given serious consideration to quality control as one of its main operating principles.

In order to establish this policy, the 'guarantee system' was adopted by which each worker in the manufacturing departments guaranteed the quality of his own work. Results in terms of quality, quantity and cost were steadily improved.

In this way, all workers became more conscious of quality and this resulted in the formation of the QC Circle movement. From the time the first circle was founded, in 1964, the movement has gained strength each year and by late 1968, there were 500 circles with more than 4,600 participants.

Sometimes workers complain that the circle in their department is rather inactive. However, the reasons for these complaints almost never are the circle members themselves. They usually result from problems concerning the training programme.

The training programme often did not encourage use and development of the individual workers' abilities and therefore workers lacked constructive thinking and attitudes. There was a want of thrust in subordinates and this did not make for a suitable environment in which the circle movement could grow.

The QC Circle movement is no short term proposition. Even if the name should change, the basic thinking which sustains the movement, i.e. the respect for autonomy, the fostering and expansion of abilities, the offering of a chance to gain knowledge, etc will never change.

It is felt that the mission imposed on those who participate in our training programme is to develop Japan's unique QC Circle movement so that it will be firmly established and last for a long time.

---

[*] Shunichi Harada is Quality Control Department Chief, Haratsuka Plant, Yokohama Rubber Co., Shinjuku, Hiratsuka City, Kanagawa Prefecture.

QUALITY CONTROL CIRCLE CASE STUDIES

In preparing the case studies introduced below, we have utilized cause-and-effect diagrams, Pareto diagrams and control charts from QC Circle reports. They do not have an established form and no deliberate use is made of QC techniques. The problems treated are highly pertinent to this plant and these studies represent marked improvements introduced by the QC Circle movement.

Case study: Reduction of cost of utilizing bag valves for tyre vulcanization

In the final manufacturing step, tyres are placed in a mould and are vulcanized by application of heat and pressure from the inside

Figure 1 Tyre with bag inserted

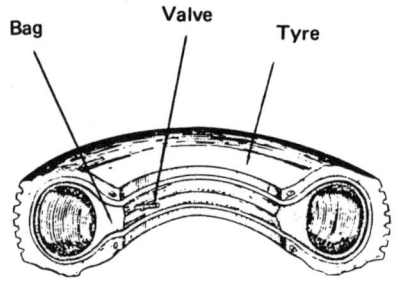

Figure 2 Valve

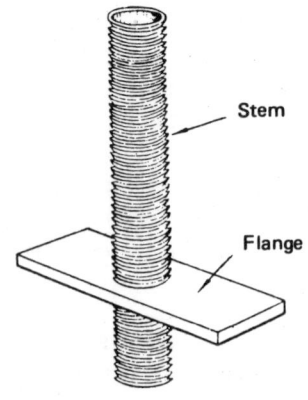

and outside simultaneously. In one method to apply heat from the inside, a rubber curing bag is inserted in the tyre and high pressure steam is forced into it. The subject for this study concerned the utilization of the brass valves used in these bags (figures 1 and 2).

Reason for choosing this subject
The function of these valves is to allow for the introduction and expulsion of steam to and from the bag. Since the bag is used over and over again for tyre vulcanization, the threads on the valve become worn, bent, or broken by repeated usage, and soon become uselsss.

Until recently, these damaged valves were merely disposed of as scrap. However, each valve is valued at 320 yen and every month 1,000 new valves were purchased at the cost of 320,000 yen ($US890). Therefore, investigations were started to find some way to reduce this cost.

Procedure
Valves were always damaged on the upper part of the stem. The flange and the part of the stem below the flange were not damaged since they are inserted inside the bag.

At first, the damaged part was cut off and a new piece was welded on in its place (figure 3). It was thought that with this method, only half of the previously required number of new valves need

Figure 3

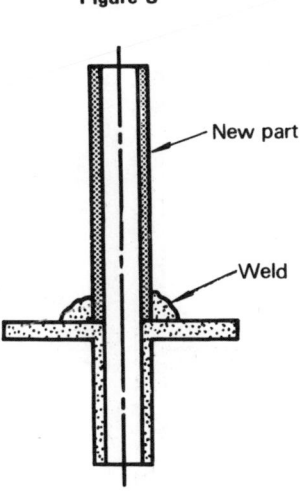

be purchased and since the repaired valves could be used many times, this would result in considerable savings. However, actual use of this method showed that the welded part was too weak, and the method had to be abandoned. In the second trial, a recess was made in the flange and the new stem was welded on (figure 4). This also proved to be too weak and had to be abandoned. In the third test, a new stem was inserted through the flange and welded to the flange. This was found to be just as effective as a new valve (figure 5).

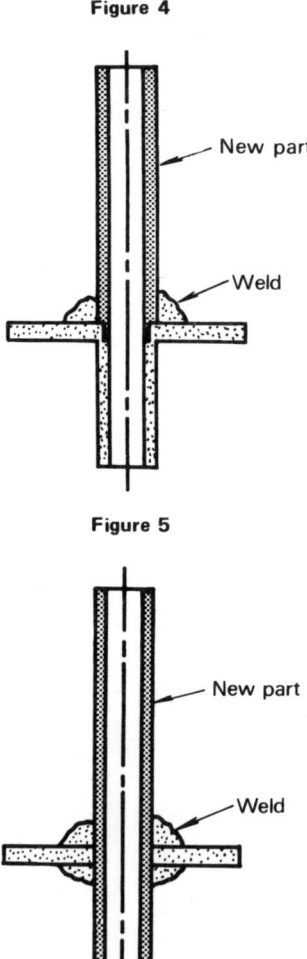

Figure 4

Figure 5

Results

With the third method, it became unnecessary to purchase the entire new valve; only new stems were needed. If this new method is used, the cost of the new stem plus the cost of welding amounts to only 150 yen, which means a saving of 170 yen on each valve or a total of 170,000 yen ($US470) a month.

Case study: Simplification of the weighing of rubber compounding ingredients

Rubber compounds used in the manufacture of rubber products are made by mixing the rubber in a mixing mill with such compounding ingredients as raw rubber, zinc white and carbon. Weighing of these compounding ingredients at the time of mixing is extremely important, but improvement in this process resulted from a simple idea.

Reason for choosing this subject

It was felt that the weighing process could be simplified by checking the compound specification sheet, or recipe. It was noted that the weight of compounding ingredient A used in one batch was very close to the weight of one bag of the material.

One bag weighed 20 kg and the amount used per batch was 19.5 kg. Therefore, if one bag was used, it became unnecessary to weigh out that compounding ingredient.

Procedure

The weight of compound A per batch used at present is shown in table 1.

As described above, the weight of the compounding ingredient becomes 20 kg, and therefore the quality section advised that the amounts of rubber and oil must also be changed accordingly.

In the quality department, investigations were carried out to see if the increases would have any mechanical effect on the mixing

Table 1 Weight of compounding ingredient

	Weight of rubber (kg)	Compounding ingredient (kg)	Oil (kg)	Total (kg)
Before improvement	40.10	19.50	0.42	60.02
After improvement	41.10	20.00	0.43	61.53

mill or would alter the characteristics of the compound. It was confirmed that there was no problem in either case and the compound specification sheet was altered as in table 1.

Results

After the improvement described above was instituted, it was no longer necessary to have personnel to weigh out compound A. With this reduction of one worker, there was also elimination of loss due to spilling of the compounding ingredient, which always occured during the weighing process.

Also, the amount of foreign matter present in the mixer was reduced, and the amount of dirt present in the shop became negligible. This improvement was thus effective beyond our original expectations.

Case 7

Replacement of intermediate inspection by independent inspection

Katsuharu Oshima[*]

As a manufacturer of lighting equipment, our company produces mercury lamps, reflector lamps, sodium vapor lamps and Xenon lamps and their stabilizers. QC Circle activities in the company are still relatively new, having started in 1967. Early QC Circle activity embodied acquiring a working knowledge of QC techniques; only recently have our efforts contributed substantially and proven their worth relative to our daily work activities.

Our 10-member group is in charge of sealing the luminous tube — the most important part of a mercury lamp. The group is composed of two Seal Circles, each of which has its own leader.

Our area of responsibility lies in sealing of the electrode mounts (shown in figure 1) from the ends of the quartz glass tube. The mount consists of main electrodes, auxiliary electrode, sealed foil, and lead wire.

Formerly, it was the usual practice for two inspectors to check the sealed tubes upon completion of sealing; this we called the intermediate inspection. Elimination of this inspection and institution of independent inspection, and reduction in the occurrence of defects in the production process, were attained through our QC Circle activity.

The advances we have made in circle activity are described below in the order of occurrence.

Building the foundation of a QC Circle

Generally, QC Circle activities contribute greatly to improvement of production process and prevention of defects during production. Moreover, the contributions towards improved human relations deserve special attention. This is the main reason we started QC

---

[*] Katsuharu Oshima is from No. 1 Production Section, Saitama Works, Iwasaki Electric Co., Gyoda City, Saitama Prefecture.

Figure 1 Structure of the luminous tube

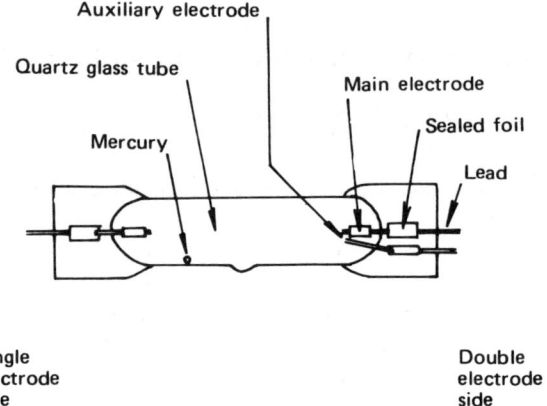

Circle activity; we wanted to build up better human relations within our company.

The first topics to be taken up were instruction in QC methodology and instruction aimed at increasing quality consciousness.

Among the QC activities, we found that knowledge of QC techniques better prepared us to approach problems. To acquaint all circle members with techniques, we used easy-to-understand slides because audio-visual aids have been found to be more effective than lecture-type classes. The person in charge of quality control provided explanations as the slides were shown. He also had printed for distribution to us simple examples of situations wherein QC techniques had been utilized in our own company. We were the first group to make use of this educational method, and once its advantages were confirmed we recommended the method to other circles.

In those early stages of QC development, what troubled us most was how to go about setting our goal. We knew, however, that once the goal was set, everyone would have to mobilize his own reserves of energy, and that when the goal was attained, everyone would likewise share in the satisfaction that arises from accomplishment.

We went about forming the habit of autonomous individual development, while at the same time establishing goals, determining the policies which had to be adhered to, and formulating a schedule. We selected appropriate themes and then began the necessary procedure to get activities started, which were, of course, carried out in accordance with the schedule we had set and were related directly to actual daily routine so that all the circle members would play as active and as positive a role as possible.

Of course, all proceeded according to the plan within which goals were established. However, for members to aggressively participate, they must not merely have good intentions but must be able to relate their circle activities to their actual work so that their interest may be aroused and maintained. Once QC Circle activities are known by all of the members achievement standards are automatically set. This produces a sense of satisfaction in each member and when the goal is attained this satisfaction is doubled.

Establishment of proper goals

It is difficult, to say the least, to lower the ratio of defective work in the sealing process if two different circles work with different goals. Following a joint conference, we proposed, and had approved, the following as our joint goals. We wanted:

1 To elevate the level of quality-mindedness to such a degree that each worker could judge product quality himself, and reduce the defect ratio of 1.5 per cent to 0.7 per cent through the setting of his individual goal.
2 Quality guarantee for the next process.
3 Total elimination of intermediate inspection, and effectuation of independent inspection by the end of March.

QC activities planning

Our practical approach was a gradual changeover to the independent inspection system while checking for defects on a step-by-step basis (figure 2). Our timetable was as follows:

Step I Interelectrode distance control (October)
Step II Measures against faulty sealed foils (November)
Step III Cultivation of independent inspection ability (December)
Step IV Testing of independent inspection (January to February)
Step V Elimination of intermediate inspection (March)

And to insure that the QC Circle would not be dissolved before achieving the goal of independent inspection, we established a set

QUALITY CONTROL CIRCLE CASE STUDIES

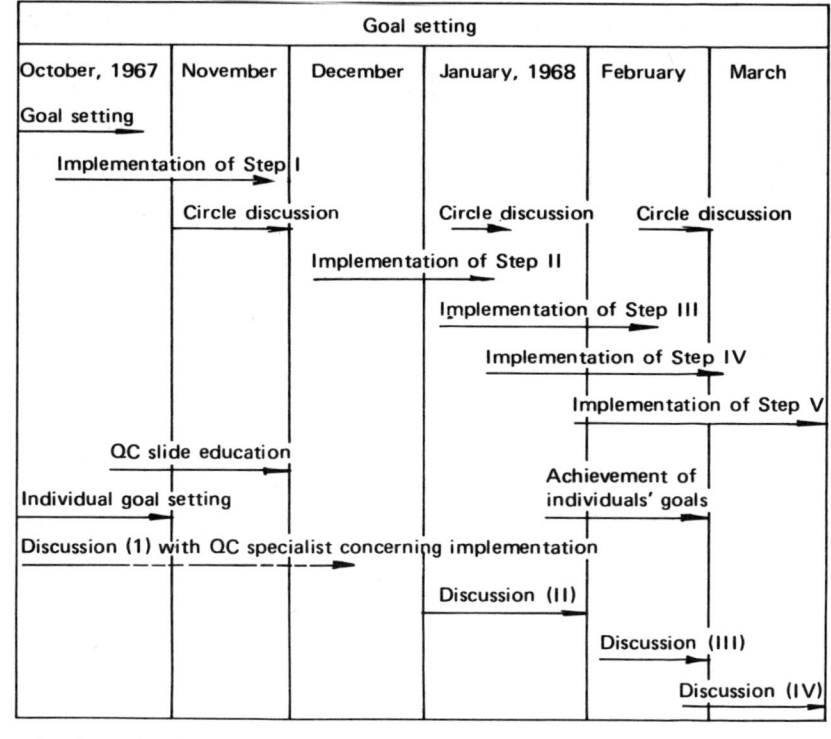

Figure 2 Independent inspection schedule

of principles by which further advance in activities could be made:
1 The circle will meet regularly on Mondays and Wednesdays, and each meeting will last at least 30 minutes.
2 Chairmanship will rotate among circle members.
3 Minutes of each meeting will be kept, and will be reported to the circle chief.
4 All members will attend the meetings.
5 All views will be held in high regard.

In addition to the five principles which we established, it was decided to make positive proposals, exchange views with other circles, make QC questionnaires, and register our QC Circles with the JUSE.

Steps effected by QC Circle activities

Step I: Interelectrode distance control

Formerly, first-piece inspection was practiced at each sealing machine to determine interelectrode distances. Data obtained by inspectors from this check were reported to the workers for necessary action. This system was replaced by the worker's individual first-piece inspection system, and the data which each worker obtained was plotted on the control chart.

This consequently made the chart workable. Because each worker was able to rapidly prepare his own data, dispersion was reduced, the next process was facilitated, so that use of this method was continued.

Step II: Against faulty sealed foils
A cause-and-effect diagram was made after several discussions. The portion of the diagram dealing with 'materials' was selected for further concentration.

Analysis revealed that the main cause was damaged ends of the sealed foil. On the basis of this, we suggested improvements in the acceptance inspection method; these improvements were made. Statistics on defects were prepared for each machine, and to the general maintenance standards were added standards derived for each machine. As a result of enforcing the standards, there was a decrease in defective sealed foils in comparison to October.

Step III: Cultivation of independent inspection ability
The intermediate inspection standards at this point were carefully examined and improvements were made by inspectors, quality inspection were established and incorporated in the work standard list. All QC Circle members were given a printed explanation of the standards for checking product defects, but at a meeting the following points were brought up by members:
1 They were not absolutely sure that independent inspection would work.
2 They felt that they would not be able to complete the predetermined work-loads.
3 They were afraid of passing defects as acceptable and causing trouble at the next process.

In view of these apprehensions, we went about setting brief rules to precludes the possibility of materialization of these fears:
1 "We must strive for the best in independent inspection."
2 "We must, as occasion demands, increase our working hours to complete the predetermined work-loads."
3 "We must learn to be objective enough to check all defectives by independent inspection."

QUALITY CONTROL CIRCLE CASE STUDIES

Step IV: Testing of independent inspection
Information concerning the inspection standard, and limits, was made available to all employees and the first test of independent inspection was made.

In accordance with the independent inspection standards, products checked by the workers were again inspected by the intermediate inspectors, to determine whether or not there were defects which had been missed. This procedure was followed for one month, after which the shift to independent inspection was made.

The result was that the defects rejected by independent inspection accounted for 82.5 per cent of the total rejects made by the inspector, a figure much better than anticipated, although 17.5 per cent of the defects went undetected. Since the inspection method was not used perfectly, only these figures were recorded. No sufficient data were available to make clear the cause of undetected defects. For this reason, the second test was arranged to last for one month. To complete the data collected in the first test, more detailed data concerning the rate of detecting defectives by each individual and undetected defectives was collected (figure 3).

The defect discovery rate in the second test was 98.6 per cent. Since items missed by individuals were easy to spot, it was easy to provide individual guidance.

Figure 3 Change in the rate of product defects before and after independent inspection

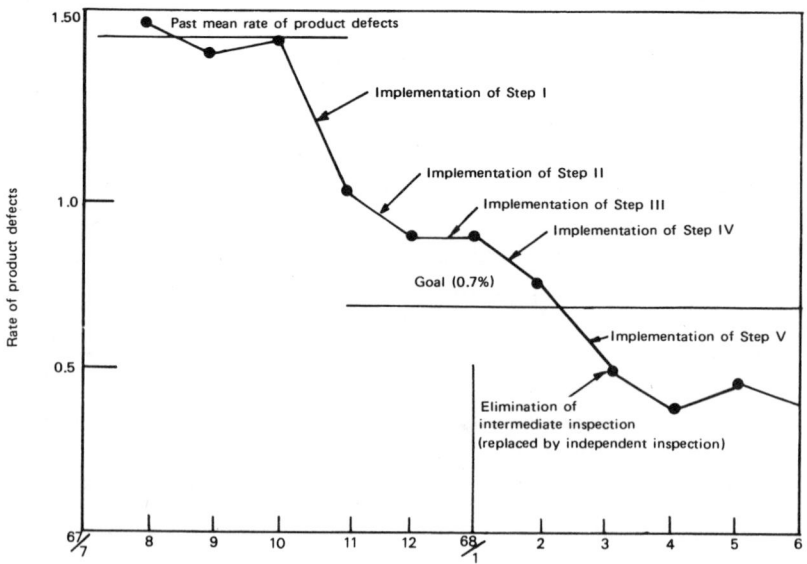

Step V: Elimination of intermediate inspection

Since we had achieved two of the three initial goals, we discussed the third goal at a regular QC Circle meeting and decided that intermediate inspection be completely abolished if no abnormality was likely to appear in inspecting finished products (figure 4).

Formal and detailed inspection conducted by the inspectors in the intermediate test with respect to lots of certain quantity before sending them to the subsequent process was alternated with a simplified inspection which was conducted by workers and included only major items and the checking of the quantities.

In this new system, the troubles or process retardation resulting from the complicated procedure undertaken only by two inspectors for all the transferring of the machines and the complete inspections have been thoroughly solved by the aid of the worker inspection. The sealing work, now included among the responsibilities of the workers, has been carried out with the same efficiency as before despite the fact that the additional burden imposed on the workers as the result of inclusion of the work inspection might cause some disadvantage to the new method. However, this has been overcome by the progress achieved in the work inspection procedures by the workers through their routine.

Convinced with this result, the manufacturer has been employing this new system, since March 25, 1968, that excludes the intermediate test inspectors and entrusts the test and the inter-process transfer of products to the workers.

Figure 4 Inspection processes before and after revision

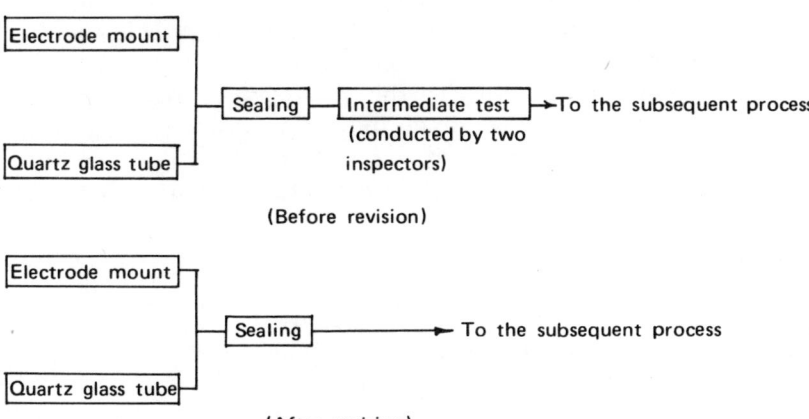

Unforeseen advantages

The success of QC Circle activities lay not only in the achievement in full measure of the initial objectives, but also in other unforeseen ways. Some of these were:

1. Interest of workers in defects was increased by the use of independent inspection and carried over into their subsequent behavior.
2. Circle members' quality consciousness was sharpened, relations with up-line and down-line processes were cemented and the ideals of quality guaranteeing took root.
3. Intermediate inspections were carried out by the worker himself. The inspection staff could thus be reduced by two, with a monthly saving of 120,000 yen in expenses including wages.
4. Bottlenecks in the production line were eliminated bringing major reductions in idle time at succeeding stages and raising efficiency.
5. Rejects were reduced by approximately two-thirds, markedly higher than the target figure (materials costs were reduced about 85,000 yen month).
6. Personal relations within the circle and with other circles were improved, making for a happier atmosphere throughout the shop.

In addition to these results there were countless other improvements, both tangible and intangible, and it may well be said that this was only possible because everyone realized and respected his own individual position, comprehended the problem that was taken up, set targets of achievement, and planned towards a final target. It is also worthy of special note that even though the inspectors were abolishing their own job, they nevertheless pushed on aggressively.

For us, it was a big topic that this very sense of cooperation was a precious aspect of the circle spirit. We learned from these achievements that 'where there's a will there's a way,' and this assures that we do have that will in our future activities. QC Circle activities are something to be conceived, considered, and implemented by all. It is better for one hundred to advance one pace than for one to go a hundred paces. I feel also that a further significance of QC Circle activities lies in the realization of the motivation and creativity latent in the members.

Case 8

Reduction of raw silk sticking

Yoshinobu Kobayashi[*]

Since 1965, the QC Circle movement became active throughout the entire company. A number of improvements have been made and one case study from the Nagai Plant is introduced below.

Purposes of the QC Circle movement

1. The movement shall carry out improvement projects on the basis of suggestions from executives and find ways to solve problems concerning development of planned projects as well as daily processing.
2. All members shall become thoroughly familiar with QC and QC thinking through study of QC principles.
3. Mutual enlightenment shall be achieved by attending intra- and inter-company QC exchange conferences and reporting case studies.

QC Circle organization

Selection of subjects
Subjects for QC Circle consideration shall concern problems which come up in plans for improvement, or which arise in connection with problems concerning implementing of plans.

QC Circle formation and activities
The leaders are to be subsection chiefs and women's group chiefs. Member are to be approved persons or persons chosen by the leader. Leaders are to devise plans for improvement in accordance with the subjects. These plans are then submitted to the pertinent section chiefs for approval. If the plans are approved, they are registered in the QC office. Planned improvement is carried out

---

[*] Yoshinobu Kobayashi is from the Technological Department, Gunze, Ltd., Nagai Plant, Nagai City, Yamagata Prefecture.

independently, on the basis of help and assistance mainly from the leaders as well as the sub-section chiefs and technical staff. If the goals are achieved and the subject problem is solved, the circle leader makes a report of the results and submits it to the section chief. These achievement reports are evaluated and awards are given to those circles which raise the level of the circle movement. The case study presented here is based on a subject which was voluntarily taken up by five persons (three men and two women) in one sub-section in November, 1966.

Case study: Reduction of raw silk sticking

The silk-reeling process is mainly concerned with combining the large number of raw silk filaments obtained from the cocoons in the previous process into one thread and winding it on small reels, A fixing agent known as sericin is added to these cocoon filaments and the large number of cocoon filaments are combined into a single thread. However, if this thread is not dried sufficiently, the threads will stick together during reeling resulting in 'raw silk sticking.' This reduces both quality and efficiency, while thread wastage increases. Raw silk sticking is especially common during winter and presented a big problem in this factory.

Reasons for selecting the subject
1 The quality of raw silk was reduced and reel cutting increased.
2 Manpower was necessary to separate the stuck thread.

Figure 1 Diagram of reeling process

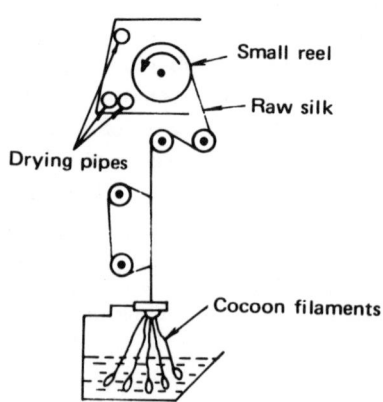

3 Waste thread increased and the thread yield rate decreased. These chronic problems were considered to be a good subject for the QC Circle to tackle.

Process outline

The process steps are: cocoon storage — cocoon selection — boiling the cocoons — cocoon distribution — finding the filament end — cocoon supply — reeling — removing the reel. During the reeling process, under consideration here, sticking occurs when the raw silk is wound on the small reels. The reels are shown in the upper part of figure 1.

Preparation of a cause-and-effect diagram

A cause-and-effect diagram was drawn up in order to determine what were the causes behind the sticking (figure 2).

Inspection for sticking

Inspections were carried out at separate times and in separate groups to find out under what circumstances sticking occurs.

Inspection of drying conditions

Since the most important factor is the extent of drying in the vicinity of the small reel, attempts were made to investigate it but direct inspection proved too difficult. Therefore, an indirect inspection-analysis (table 1) was carried out.

Comparison of sticking in different groups

A Pareto diagram to investigate the number of times sticking occured in each group is shown in figure 3.

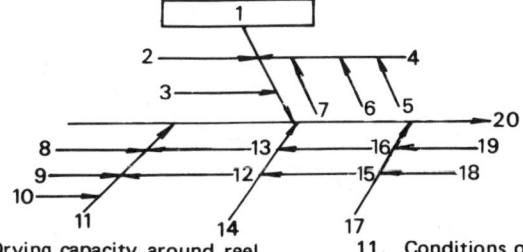

Figure 2 Cause-and-effect diagram for raw silk sticking

1. Drying capacity around reel
2. Steam pressure
3. Velocity of hot air
4. Temperature and humidity in shop
5. Outside temperature and humidity
6. Climate
7. Skylight opening
8. Reeled thread temperature and moisture content
9. Cocoon boiling
10. Materials
11. Conditions of reeled thread
12. Twisting
13. Reel speed
14. Removal from reel
15. Speed
16. Amount of hot water
17. Reel temperature
18. Temperature in shop
19. Wet reel
20. Raw silk sticking

QUALITY CONTROL CIRCLE CASE STUDIES

Whether or not the occurrence of sticking varies among the groups was investigated by means of a goodness-of-fit test, and it was revealed that the valves measured were significantly different. However, except for group No. 7, there were no really significant differences. A check of the drying tubes of group No. 7 revealed a defect and this was fixed.

Comparison of sticking at different times
Since sticking occurred very often in winter, it was felt that the

Table 1 inspection of drying conditions

Month/day	Time	Climate	Outside temperature	Steam pressure	Amount of sky-light opening	Thermometer I (To the south)			Thermometer II (In the centre)			Thermometer III (To the north)		
						Dry bulb	Wet bulb	Temperature	Dry bulb	Wet bulb	Temperature	Dry bulb	Wet bulb	Temperature
12/15	6	Cloudy	−1°C	3.7 km/cm²	50%	24	20	64	27	22	59	26	21	58
	9	"	1 "	4.5 "	100%	26	21	58	28	22	53	28	22	53
	12	"	6 "	3.5 "	"	29	24	60	31	24	50	30	24	55
	15	"	6 "	4.5 "	"	30	24	55	35	24	52	31	25	56
	18	"	4 "	4.5 "	"	32	24	45	34	26	47	33	25	46
	21	"	3 "	5.0 "	"	31	24	50	33	24	42	33	24	42

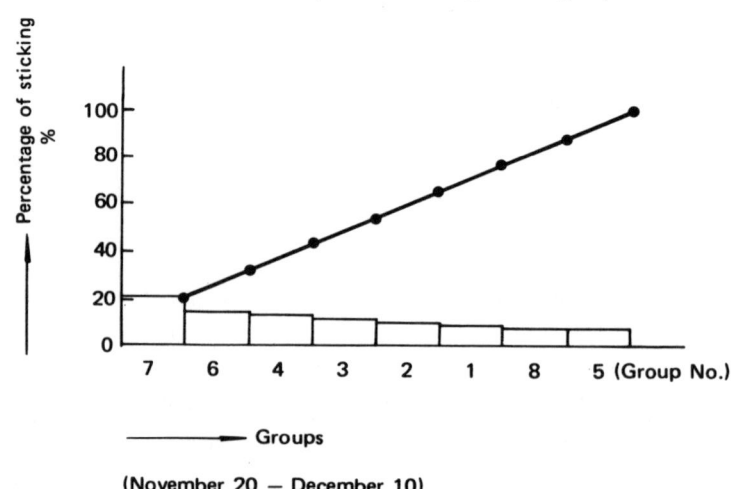

Figure 3 Pareto diagram for sticking in each group

(November 20 − December 10)

outside temperature had some effect. Daily checks were made at regular intervals during the day shift and also during the afternoon and night shifts and it was found that sticking was more frequent

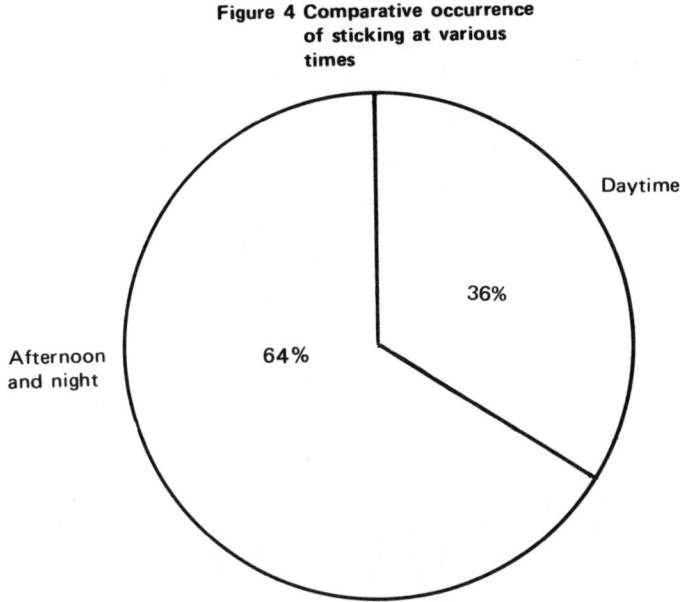

Figure 4 Comparative occurrence of sticking at various times

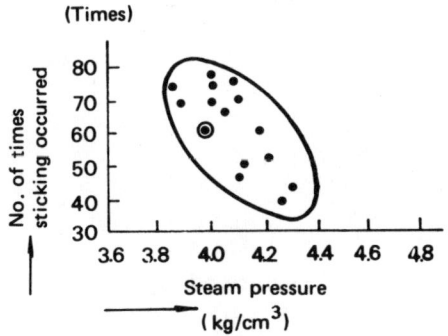

Figure 5 Scatter diagram for steam pressure and occurrence of sticking

No. of measurements by correlation test: n = 17,
$r = -0.498$
$|r| > r(15, 0.05) = 482$

Figure 6 Occurrence of sticking after improvement

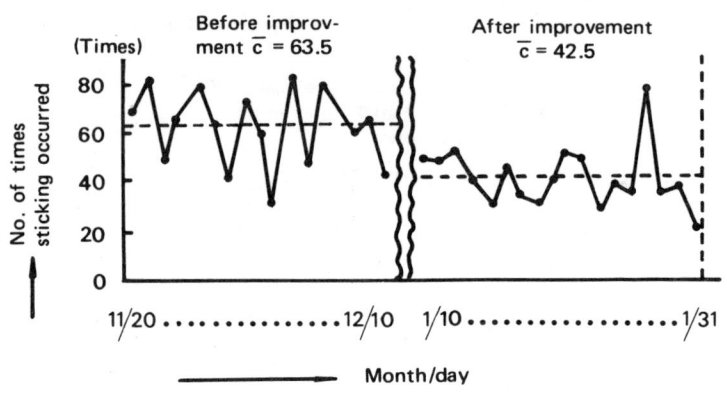

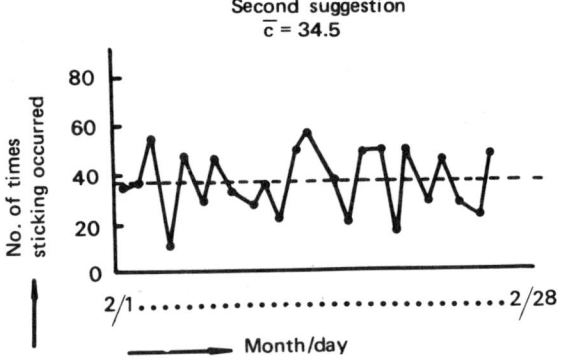

during the afternoon and night shifts when the temperature was lower (figure 4).

Relation between steam pressure and sticking
In contrast to the investigations of drying and sticking, sticking occurred very often when the steam pressure was low. A scatter diagram was compiled as shown in figure 5.

A correlation test was performed to find out the correlation coefficient and the correlation between the two factors was evident.

Two alternative plans were suggested for improvement (figure 6). The first plan was to raise steam pressure to 4.5 kg/cm² when the outside temperature is over 5°C and increase steam pressure to 4.8 kg/cm² when outside temperature is 5°C or below.

Standardization and results
Since the mean value difference between the two alternative plans was significantly large, the second plan was standardized.

The results were as follows:
1. Waste thread and labour were reduced which resulted in a saving of 30,000 yen (US$83) per month.
2. Indirectly, the quality was improved considerably (the claims of split threads were brought to almost nil).

The occurrence of sticking has been reduced but it has not yet been reduced sufficiently. Since the steam pressure cannot be raised above the new values, a reel cover made of heat insulating materials is being considered as a measure for further improvement.

Case 9

Reduction of defective soldering work in assembling electrical appliances

Akira Kato[*]

Well-co-ordinated QC group activities

At Hitachi, QC group activities are not always called QC Circle activities. QC Circle activities have received such widespread publicity that they have become very important at most of our 22 factories throughout Japan. At some factories, ZD (Zero Defect) projects, which include QC activities, are employed.

Although the name of programmes may differ from factory to factory, there is only one objective: to instill in the mind of each worker the desire to reduce defective work to as close to zero as possible.

Company-wide guidelines for QC Circle activity have been announced. Much progress has been made at individual factories in keeping with our president's policy of "reducing management losses caused by defective work and improving management conditions in the factory."

QC Circle activities at Hitachi may be defined as follows: "With the objective of elevating quality consciousness in the plants so that quality can be guaranteed and manufacturing costs reduced, to organize groups of employees and let them act autonomously."

"To elevate quality consciousness" means that each employee recognizes the importance of his role and his job, knows that quality depends upon himself; and exerts all possible efforts to improve quality.

"So that quality can be guaranteed and manufacturing costs reduced" means that all personnel concerned with quality strive to guarantee satisfactory functions and performance of the products from the viewpoint of the user and to reduce manufacturing costs through improving manufacturing processes.

---

[*] Akira Kato is from the Taga Factory, Hitachi Ltd., Hitachi City.

"Act autonomously" means that although organizational support is indispensable, the activities essentially must be autonomous and continuous, and must expand through active cooperation of the group members.

QC Circle activities at the Taga factory

At the Taga factory, which has colour television production lines, more than 5,800 workers produce 4,500,000,000 yen (US$12,500,000) worth of household appliances, general-purpose motors, and industrial equipment monthly.

Birth of QC Circle

In keeping with the plant manager's policy, "to be active on the international scene on the basis of assured quality," the training of foremen and trainers in quality control was begun several years ago. QC Circles at this factory were born through the trainees' eager desire to learn by applying the lectures to problems actually encountered in production.

At the beginning, there were 13 QC Circles, organized by 70 foremen at the Taga factory. To establish a beachhead where QC is concerned in the field of manufacturing, the supervisors must first fully understand the meaning of QC and become thoroughly familiar with its methods; this has been realized.

Reorganization of QC Circles

It was recognized that the QC Circles, originally meant as an extension of training for foremen, were a most valuable means of meeting demands for high quality of manufactured products, and to make the circles more effective in insuring product quality, they were reorganized into 43 new QC Circles with a few circles for each manufacturing section. An organization chart is shown in figure 1. Major personnel of the organization are supervisors and foremen. Subcircles (one per operation shop for a total of 167) have been organized into action groups, with the members of QC Circles as leaders of subcircles.

Defects reduction committee

The Defect Reduction Committee directs only the broad aspects of factory policy and does not directly manage the QC Circles. However, at the monthly meetings of the circle leaders, status

REDUCTION OF DEFECTIVE SOLDERING WORK

Figure 1 Organization chart of OC Circles

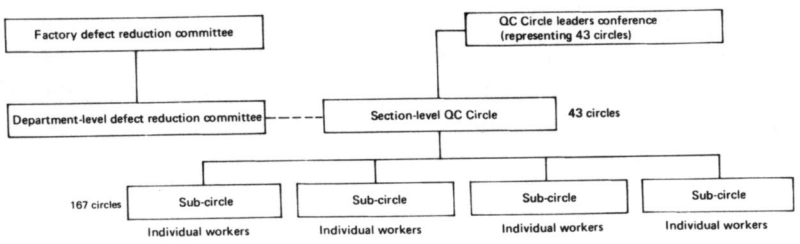

Figure 2 Types of soldering operations

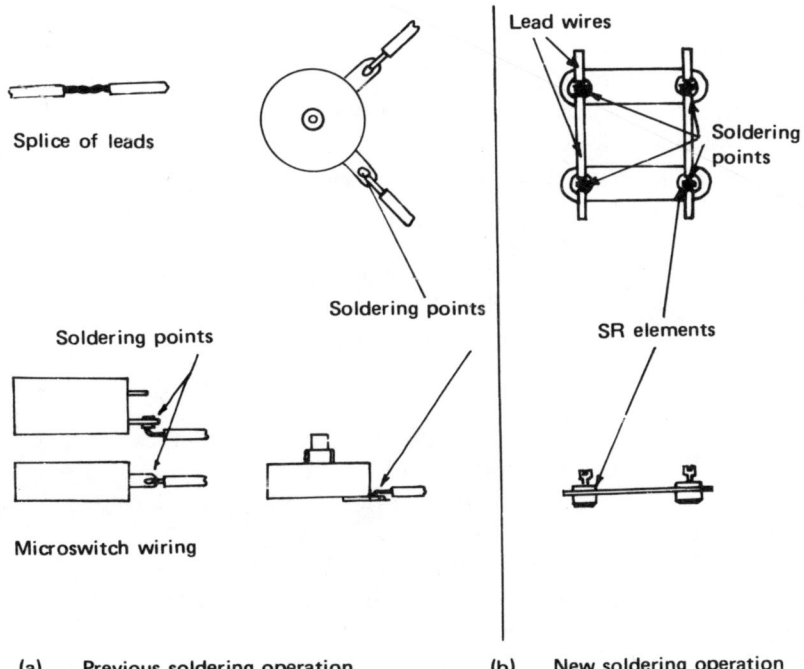

(a)　Previous soldering operation　　(b)　New soldering operation

reports and discussions are made on circle management and activities. From the viewpoint of autonomous circle activities, assistance is given only as secondary support from section leaders and persons in charge.

To insure that activities are continuous and are expanded, responsibilities for supervisors and workers are clearly demarcated. The improvement proposal adopted in a QC Circle is not limited to the circle alone but is applied also to similar operations and to other circles.

Activities of QC Circles

Activities of the QC Circles at this factory can be summarized as follows:
1. Themes determined by individual circle members in turn are taken up. Discussions are held once or twice monthly.
2. Discussions are held on how to prevent everyday defects and countermeasures are implemented.
3. Reading of the monthly publication *QC for the Foreman* and other source material to enlighten personnel in method used to solve problems.
4. Meetings are held by each circle or section to summarize the effects of group activities. QC Circle reports are submitted.
5. Exchanges are carried out with nearby factories. Circle members attend nationwide QC Circle conferences whenever possible.
6. A meeting of circle leaders is held monthly. Reports on circles' activities, exchange of information, and follow-up activities are made at this meeting.
7. Technicians in charge of QC in the individual manufacturing sections assist QC Circles. The Planning Office provides guidance and support on QC for the factory as a whole.

Effects of QC Circles

The ultimate objective of the QC activities is to let each worker in the field realize the importance of quality control and to provide him with a knowledge of QC. The following effects have already been realized:
1. Defective work has been reduced and yield rates improved.
2. Proposals for improvement are now actively and freely submitted.
3. Reduction in working processes has been realized through autonomous action, resulting in reduction of costs.

DEFECTIVE SOLDERING WORK

4 It was realized that new and improved QC techniques are readily accepted in the field.
5 Appreciation of the importance of quality has been instilled in the workers, who now eagerly study QC methods.
6 Liaison between group members has improved, resulting in an improvement in human relations.
7 Instructions to workers are conveyed quicker and morale has been improved.

Case study: Reduction of defective soldering of parts of mixers and juicers

Increase in defects provides motive to improve quality

The rate of assembly defects increased when production was rapidly expanded and model changes were implemented. The specific point where defective work appeared was during soldering, particularly of semi-conductors, where operator errors are likely to occur. The problem was handled by an eight-man circle..

Analysis of existing conditions and investigation of causes

Through an analysis of defective assemblies which was started in February, 1967, by the QC Circle, it was made clear, as shown in the Pareto diagram (figure 3), that the major problem was how to reduce soldering defects, which accounted for 40 per cent of all assembly defects.

For further investigation, a cause-and-effect diagram shown in figure 4 was drawn and studied by the QC Circle.

Corrective measures

Possible causes were extracted from the cause-and-effect diagram, and investigated. Corrective measures were studied by all related

Figure 3 Pareto diagram for assembly defects

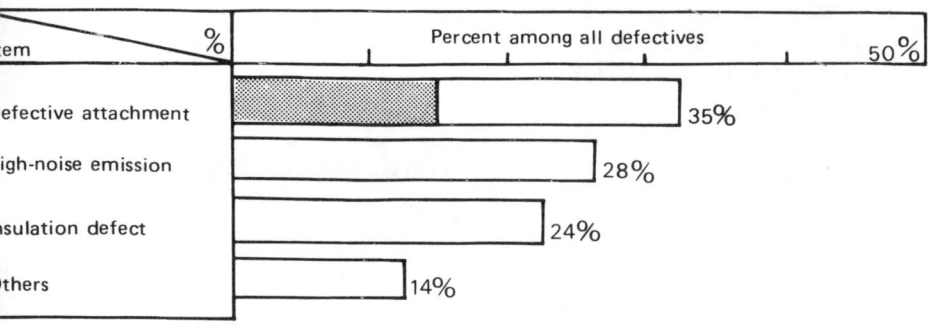

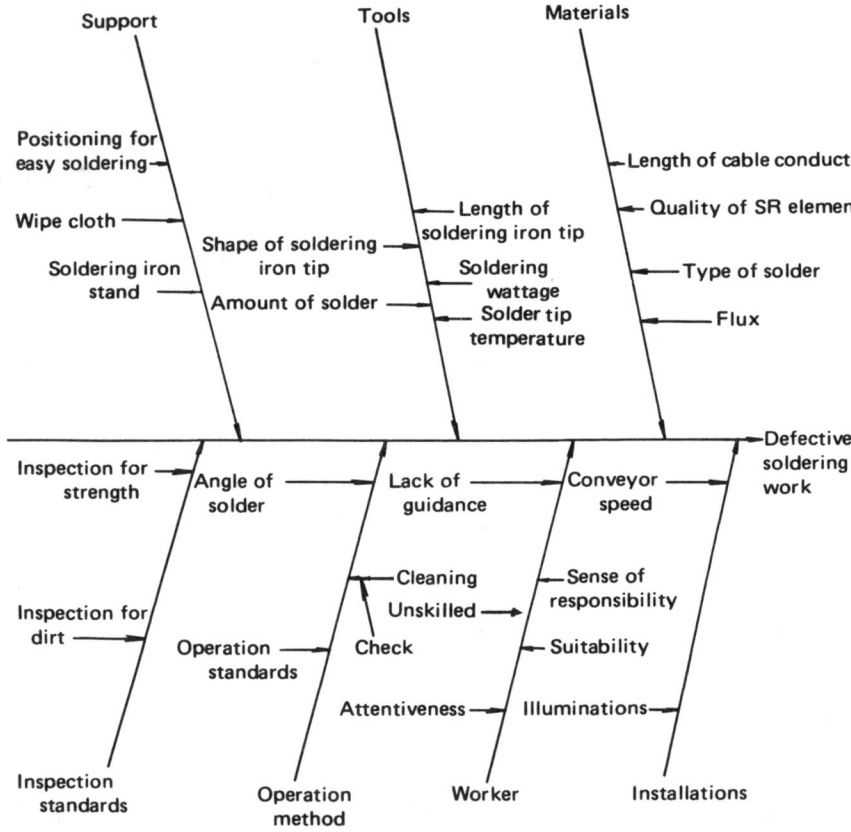

Figure 4 Cause-and-effect diagram on defective soldering works

personnel. Measures which could be readily translated into action by the individual workers were immediately implemented. For measures which required the cooperation of related groups, the concerned parties were requested to attend the QC Circle meetings and extend their active cooperation. Some of the corrective measures taken were as follows:

1. Improvement of tools: The tools were slanted so that the solder would hold better.
2. Uniform amount of solder: Provision was made so that the amount of solder would always be uniform. The soldering iron was filed every half hour to insure that the tip would be even.
3. Changes in the shape and length of soldering iron tip: The tip was made slim so that solder would flow better.

REDUCTION OF DEFECTIVE SOLDERING WORK

4 Selection of workers: Workers were classified according to skill, into three classes; only the best class's workers were assigned to soldering.

5 Temperature control of the soldering iron tip: Temperature was adjusted with a transformer four times a day.

6 Use of flux: Quality flux was used. Soldered connections were cleaned.

7 Improvement of illumination: Illumination was improved at 10 places.

8 Complete self-checking: The mechanical strength of the soldered point was checked by a pull of 2 kgs, and defects were controlled with control charts.

Effects of circle activities
As the above corrective measures were implemented starting with those which could be immediately realized the defective soldering work has been reduced to nil, as shown in figure 5.

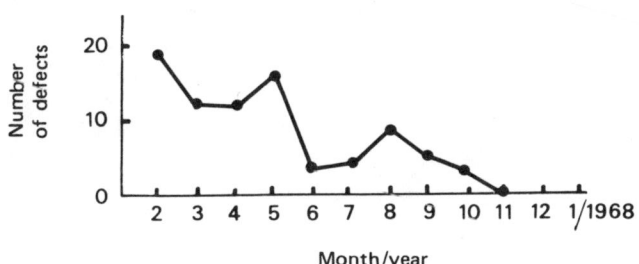

Figure 5 Reduction in defective soldering work

Case 10

Taking the leadership in quality control

Shoji Waga*

This company was founded in 1935 for commercialization of ferrite. Based on the company motto, 'Contribution to World Culture and Industry through Creativity,' we are contributing to development of the electronics industry through production of ferrite, magnetic condensers, magnetic tapes and other components of electronic devices. The company decided in 1963 that the quality control system would have to be thoroughly examined out of the desire to build a sound structure to match the economic environment which was becoming unfavourable due to trade liberalization and other factors. Accordingly, in 1965, Total Quality Control was introduced. Our QC Circle movement as presented here forms parts of TQC practiced in the main plant in Akita and was initiated in 1966. All plant personnel participate in the movement for managerial improvement of the company.

Goals of the QC Circle Movement

The Akita factory is located in Okita prefecture in northern Honshu, quite far from the industrial areas of Kanto and Kansai. The plant has 2,300 employees, most of whom are from the area where the plant is located. About half the employees are women and 370 of them are married, which is an extremely high percentage when compared with any similar figure in the rest of the country.

In order to keep up with the many technical innovations made in the electronics industry, we were required to leave behind the easy-going mood which had prevailed in our plant, and train and guide the employees so that they could use self-discipline and make their own judgements.

---

* Shoji Waga is of the Control Dept. Electronic Materials Center, Akita Plant, Tokyo Electronics Co.

QUALITY CONTROL CIRCLE CASE STUDIES

The QC Circle movement has proceeded with this in mind. The main goals of the QC Circle movement can be summarized as follows.

Enhancement of shop morale
In all the shops, groups were formed to further the QC programme. This resulted in promotion of teamwork, improvement of human relations and enhancement of shop morale.

Contribution toward management development of the company
When all shops workers study their own problems, provide their own solutions, and improve their own methods, it follows that they can do their jobs with much more ease with the improved methods, contributing toward management development of the company as a whole.

Self-study
All workers, through study of QC methods and techniques, can attain self-development as well as mutual enlightenment through exchange of views at QC Circle conferences, exchange meetings, etc. The shop workers then cease to be isolated and are able to have a broader outlook.

Quality assurance
If the movement results in improvement of shop problems, maintenance of standards, and thorough implementation of control measures, the personnel working at following production processes, and the customers, will be assured of quality.

Characteristics of induction of QC Circle movement
When the QC Circle movement was introduced care was taken, as much as possible, to have the employees form circles voluntarily and work independently. In keeping with this policy, circle formation specifications, programme regulations, etc were not formulated for the company as a whole at first. East shop was allowed to handle things as it saw fit.

As a result, each shop came up with original plans. In some shops the circle leaders were chosen by the employees from among themselves, questionnaires were distributed, newsletters were printed, morning or evening study groups were formed, and so on. With each shop setting its own individual mood, the movement became quite lively from the very beginning.

Along with this mood, the QC Circle way of thinking gradually became established and from this time on leaders' and members' training, progress report meetings, etc were instituted.

An outline of these is given below.

QC Circle training and guidance
Training

Lecture meetings: As the QC mood became established, circle leaders who were beginning to get results were invited to attend lecture meetings in order to acquaint them with ways to promote the movement. The lecturers at these meetings were young women of about 20 who discussed such pertinent problems as "how to prevent errors due to carelessness" and "what are the essential points of our own work." They made unrelenting efforts to improve their own work and so created considerable enthusiasm.

Publication of a handbook: Later a 'Handbook for the QC Circle movement' was compiled for use in leader training and all the leaders underwent this training. The contents of the handbook were as follows:

Definition of the QC Circle (circle aims, points concerning circle operation, results, etc)

Background of the QC Circle movement

How to promote circle activities (circle formation, registration procedure, programme goals, how to draw up programmes, how to lead meetings, programme checks, how to confirm results, etc)

How to make improvements (rules for resolving problems, etc)

Intra-circle activities (procedure for attending conferences, exchanges, etc)

Guidance in concrete methods of increasing circle activity.

Members meetings: After the leaders training was finished, a training course was given three times each month for about 60 circle members at a time. The course lasted for four hours.

The curriculum consisted of a slide presentation and lectures on QC Circles, exchanges of views with plant executives, and evaluations, as voiced by participants.

The course served as a base for the effective spread of knowledge. Of the 2,000 people who intended to take the course, about 25 per cent had completed it by late 1968.

Subscribing to the QC *for the Foreman:* When the movement was introduced, encouragement was given to subscribe to the magazine QC *for the Foreman.* As the movement gained momentum this increased and by late 1968 290 copies were being sent to the factory every month. Since there are 197 circles in our company, each circle uses 1.5 issues.

To facilitate utilization of this magazine, a 'Utilization Guide' is printed every month when the magazine arrives at the plant and everyone is encouraged to read it.

Publication of a company magazine on QC: In addition to subscribing to *QC for the Foreman,* a company QC Circle organ, 'Circle Forum' is being printed to increase the workers' knowledge of the movement and promote closer connections between the circles.

This contains an introduction of circles, impressions of QC functions, conferences, exchange meetings, etc; information on how to use simple techniques, requests concerning the circle programme, opinions, company topics, etc. It is edited by circle members on an alternating basis and may be amateurish but it does contain material of interest to the workers.

Learning QC techniques through lectures: QC training courses are held within the company as one fact of the TQC programme. These courses deal with basic QC principles, control charts, and statistics. They are given after working hours by company lecturers and anyone can participate. Participation is high and 360 people have already completed the basic course. These courses are highly effective in promoting the utilization of techniques related to the circle movement.

Reports of circle results and intra-circle activities
Monitoring the movement: The general conditions at the time of the circle meetings are reported in the 'Minutes of QC Circle Meetings' and the circles which have made achievements print a report on them. Both are circulated to shop chiefs, and are included in the 'Monthly Circle Report' put out by each section.

The office staff gives advice as required concerning these publications.

QC Circle conferences in the plant: Circles are given a chance once every three months to report results they have attained at the plant QC Circle conference. This conference is organized by circle members, and plant chiefs are encouraged to attend as judges or commentators. These conferences are held on non-working days. Attendance is voluntary, and has steadily increased.

Inter-plant conferences: Besides the plant QC Circle conference, an all-company QC conference is held every six months.

Since there are many married women in this plant, a 'Working Woman's Meeting' is held for them. A 'QC Circle progress report meeting' is held for the staff in charge of day-to-day guidance and training of the QC Circles. Each of these meetings has a different viewpoint, but they all serve very effectively to bring about improvements.

Attendance at QC circle conferences outside the company: The All-Japan QC Circle Conference is held at various locations throughout the country by the Union of Japanese Scientists and Engineers. Workers from our plant attend these conferences every two months.

Up to and including the Sapporo Conference in July, 1967, members simply attended without actively participating. However, reports were submitted at the later Toyama Conference and 15 reports have been given since then.

Attending these conferences and giving reports is naturally self-enlightening and is a good opportunity to build self-confidence, which makes these people even more effective when they return.

Exchanging experiences with other companies: In July, 1967, the first of these meetings was held with the Electrical Appliance Parts Department of Matsushita Electric Co. and since then five such meetings have been held.

Figure 1

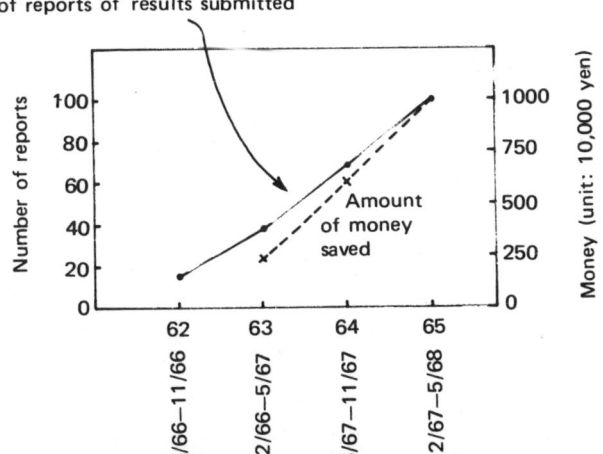

It is also felt that there are many opportunities for self-improvement through exchanges with other companies during the QC conference.

Achievement awards

The reports submitted by circles who have made some definite achievements are checked by the office and a commendation and prize are awarded to a successful reporter during the monthly all-factory morning assembly. This award, irrespective of the money saved by the improvement, is only about 300 yen (less than US$1) per person, but serves as an incentive to the circle movement.

Monthly awards are very often given for tangible achievements but the circle movement also encourages intangible achievements such as elevation of morale. For this reason intangible results are also included in the office staff's deliberations concerning circle activity. A yearly award is made on the company's founding day.

Overall results

Direct Achievements

The direct achievements of the circle movement are indicated in figure 1.

These results are calculated for six-month periods and in January, 1968 they reached 100 reported cases for a savings of 10,000,000 yen (US$27,800).

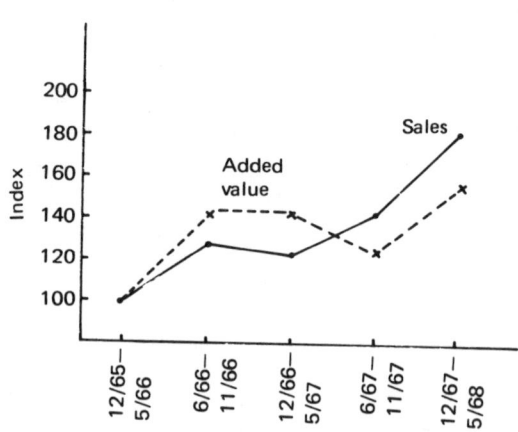

Figure 2 Sales and value added per person

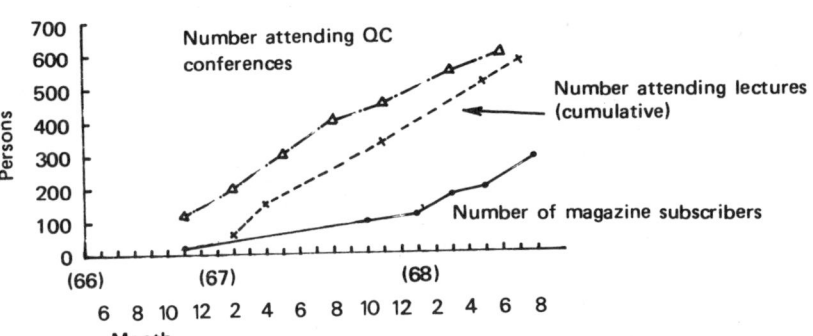

Figure 3 General conditions concerning voluntary attendance at QC activities

In our company, direct results were not considered to be the most important. We have always had faith that the movement would produce results, and as the movement progressed, the results could gradually improve. Anything contributing to this progress is deemed worthy of support.

Sales and added value per person are shown in figure 2, indicating the progress of the movement since its introduction.

We have established a highly autonomous movement and some of the indirect results of this are, for example, as follows. Married women gather at 6.30 every morning for a study group meeting; mastery of QC techniques has been amply reflected in the circle movement; incentives are given to young unmarried women; and there has been remarkable improvement of the morale of women employees (especially married women) through constructive participation in QC circle conferences, aims, etc.

circle conferences, aims, etc.

In the future, competition in quality of products will become more and more pronounced. As in the saying first come, first served,' taking the leadership in quality depends on whether the company's 'character' can be strengthened.

The QC Circle movement is one way of strengthening the company's character and therefore, it will become much more important in the future.

Case 11

Early operation of newly installed machinery
Tatsuya Yoshida*

Recently, there has been rapid expansion of sealed compressor production. Unfavourable conditions have appeared in connection with the introduction of new plant equipment and the rapid increase in new personnel. Here, we would like to introduce an example in which under favourable conditions daily quotas were filled and at the same time personnel were trained and new lines put into operation. This was accomplished by the Deming Cycle of 'Plan, Do, Check and Act.' The continued repetition of this process, which forms the basis of quality control, was the source of these results.

The origin of QC Circles
Conditions in section
Our section was organized in July, 1962, for production of Mitsubishi—Tecumseh sealed compressors. At first, the number of workers and the number of units produced were small, involving only one model, the JAE-1. Although there was an intermediate period of sluggishness, figure 1 does indicate that the number of workers and amount of production rose steadily. These compressors came to be used in various refrigeration and air conditioning equipment. There are now six basic models and 80 types.

A new factory was completed in the fall of 1968, and was scheduled to go into production early in 1969. Our work team belonging to the machining subsection, consists of 23 people whose duty it is to machine crankcases for the JCL, JAH, JAJ and JAT model compressors.

---

* Tatsuya Yoshida is Squad Chief, Machining Subsection, Biwajima Compressor Machinery Section, Nagoya Machinery Works, Mitsubishi Heavy Industries, Ltd., Nagoya

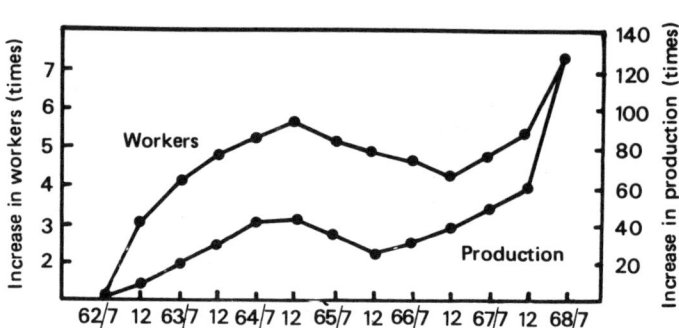

Figure 1 Increase in the number of units produced and personnel

QC Circle activities

The QC Circle in our section was founded in 1964, including the entire section, from work team foremen to 18 subordinates. Its main emphasis was on educational activities, and since that time it has grown and been divided into some 20 groups on a work team or squad basis. The writer's circle is called the Yoshida's Squad QC Circle, and consists of all 23 members of the team.

Depending on circumstances, analysis of problems may be made by five- or six-man groups. Topics are taken up first from the point of view of production and then of training, safety, and other aspects. Liaison is cemented during morning and afternoon gatherings and a meeting of approximately two hours duration is held at least once a month.

Case study: Early operation of newly installed machinery

Problems taken up

Model JCL, the largest sealed compressor, was formerly produced in small quantities: it was made to be used both for special and general purposes. In order, however, to satisfy the market demand, it was decided to rapidly expand production and to do this the works was equipped with its first transfer machine. Since this was the first time that any of the workers had had experience with this

EARLY OPERATION OF NEWLY INSTALLED MACHINERY

Figure 2 Cause and effect diagram

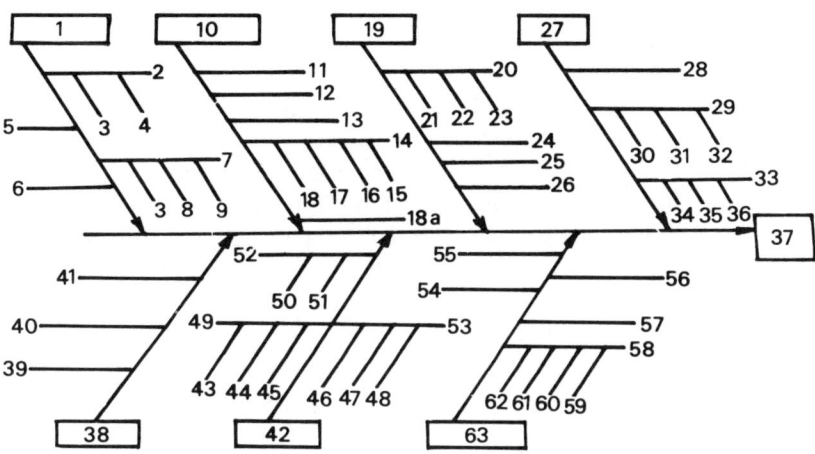

Note: There are many other causes, only the most important have been listed.

1. Electrical
2. Limit switch malfunction
3. Entry of water
4. Operational fault
5. Poor contacting
6. Faulty operation due to insulation failure
7. Faulty selonoid valve
8. Seized
9. Deterioration
10. Mechanical accuracy
11. Core eccentricity caused by the cutting unit
12. Off-levelling
13. Stopper slippage
14. Eccentricity due to vibration
15. Razor wear
16. Play in moving
17. Loose bearings
18. Sluggish movement
18a. Lack of power
19. Worker
20. Faulty mounting
21. Reference surface
22. Not checked yet
23. Not yet tightened
24. Dimensional variations
25. Mis-installation of tools
26. Faulty workmanship
27. Castings
28. Return scraps and cavities unchecked and shags unremoved
29. Scatter of accuracy
30. Pieces cut in sizes bigger than standard ones
31. Mold shift
32. Core eccentricity
33. Unacceptable reference surface
34. To M-jig
35. To one TR
36. To two TR
37. Reject case
38. Cutting fluid
39. Rusting due to incorrect concentration
40. Unsuitable (therefore heavy wear)
41. Insufficient clearance of shavings
42. Pallet (for clutching steel)
43. Meter breakage
44. Lowering of base pressure
45. Miscoupling
46. Pipe breakage
47. Gasket failure
48. Entry of water
49. Loosening due to insufficient |pressure
50. Vertical
51. Bed surface
52. Improper balance of force
53. Faulty hydraulic cylinder
54. Unacceptable guide bush
55. Unsuitable material
56. Unacceptable slipping
57. Faulty arbor
58. Defects rechecked
59. Chipping of cutting tool
60. Drill breakage
61. Tap breakage
62. Number mounted
63. Tools and jigs

QUALITY CONTROL CIRCLE CASE STUDIES

type of machine, the first thing that was necessary was to expend every effort in learning the capabilities of the machines and to train operators.

In checking how to maintain and improve the quality of crankcases while processing them, we came face to face with a number of problems. In the belief that the beginning is important, efforts were made to effect early solutions to these problems, and to this end we enlisted the cooperation of the QC Circle members as well as that of those in charge of related fields, and began planning and analysis.

Action in Production Planning

It was decided that in production planning for the transfer machine, the following action should be taken step by step, as follows:

1. To establish liaison between the metal working tool section charged with transfer machine operations and the production engineering section charged with planning, and to come to grips with problems arising during adjustments.
2. To clarify steps taken in trial machining and to process data.
3. To select, educate, and train transfer machine operators.
4. To grasp, analyze, and take countermeasures against over-all problem points involved in initiating production.

Analysis of problems

Since the author had been fortunate enough to have participated in discussions from the design and production phases, he was able to develop his own plans. This was found very useful in carrying

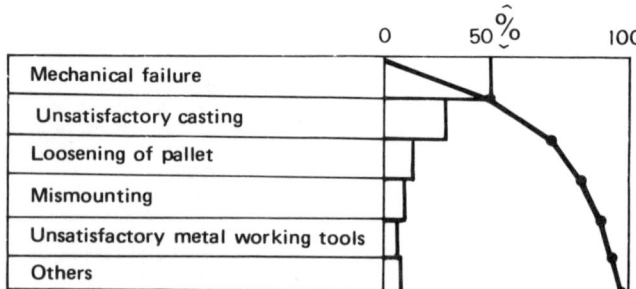

Figure 3 Pareto diagram by causes

out the measures listed below. The following points involve steps 2, 3, and 4 above.

Checks at trial machining stage
1   Variation between dispersion in castings and processing standards.
2   Precision of machines which determine product precision.
3   Reliability of machines under continuous operation.
4   Differences between projected cycle time and actual cycle time.
5   Method of operating machining tools, measures against breakdown, and preventive maintenance.

Collection of data for starting production
The following data were systematically obtained at the initial testing stage. Results are shown in the test operation column of figure 2.
1   Processing accuracy
2   Changing tools and time required to measure dimensions
3   Machine breakdown.

In connection with processing accuracy (machining), production was divided into four classes on the basis of the importance of parts characteristics, and dispersion was investigated.

Primary improvement
Various problems became apparent after the previously described investigations. The author and six workers formed a small group which held brainstorming sessions based on the collected data to study, from various angles, weak points of areas which were in need of improvement. The opinions which were then expressed were submitted to superiors along with the data and used to effect primary improvement.

Preparing a worker's guide
While these improvements were being made, data from test operations as well as the opinions and desires of the circle members were all taken into consideration and the following three standards were established.
Checking standards: These standards divided areas of checking responsibility among installation, intermediate, and disassembly personnel. It divided all characteristics into four classes on the basis of relevance to quality. These were characteristics which have

a particularly strong effect on performance (14); secondary characteristics (15); appearance and visual appeal (11).

It was further decided that it was necessary to raise the effectiveness of checking by determining the speed of checking and method of recording and taking into consideration points checked by different workers and balancing of the frequency of checking.

Tool replacement standards: Numerical data regarding safety were made available. Tool wear was expressed numerically, in order to clarify standards for changing each type of tool at each station before breakage occurred.

Preventive maintenance standards: Methods of checking precision, and conditions of lubrication, were established in order to reduce the occurrence of emergencies, particularly in relation to electrical equipment.

These standardization proposals, somewhat modified in accordance with data gained from primary improvement were then submitted to the production engineering section for consideration and formal implementation.

No decrease in rejects after improvement

Despite the great efforts which were made, the rate of rejects continued at the same level even after primary improvements were implemented. All personnel concerned realized that this was because their technical knowledge and experience with the machine was insufficient and that this in turn had led to emphasis being placed on the wrong points. This failure spurred us to undertake a second programme of improvement.

Further measures

By the time two months had elapsed after the start of production, the writer and workers had become familiar with the transfer machine and had, by implementing primary and secondary improvements, made progress in correcting the problems discovered in the first phase and in lowering the reject rate. At this time there was further discussion, countermeasures, and improvements against the causes of defects. We utilized meetings, analysis of post-improvement data, cause-and-effect diagrams and Pareto diagrams (see figure 3).

Here, I would like to deal with the most important corrective action taken.

EARLY OPERATION OF NEWLY INSTALLED MACHINERY

Figure 4 Table of results

		March 10 to 31 Test operation	April 5 to 30 after primary improvements	May 6 till July 31 after Secondary improvements	Remarks
Machining accuracy	Cylinder bore ID (inside diameter)	(curve)	(curve)	(curve)	In test-cutting steel, there was a big scatter of accuracy due to great abrasion of the cutting machine. This was improved (after April 3) by substitution of air for cutting fluid.
	Pitch of lower mounting surface	(curve)	(curve)	(curve)	This was stabilized by improvement of pallet loosening only.
Time required to attain dimensions for replacement of tools		(graph, 3/12–3/20)	(graph, 4/1–4/20)	(graph, 5/10–6/10–7/10)	Time rose in early May due to increased production, but fell after mid-May through method improvement.
Mechanical failure (monthly average)	Electrical	8	13	5	
	Hydraulic	13	Limits unacceptable 5	1 Caused by core eccentricity	
	Steel carrying and transfer (by the clutching pallet)	2	8	1	
	Cutting unit	6	1	1	
	Others	3	6 Loosening of pallet pressure	0	
	Total	32	31	9	
Variation in rate of defects		(graph %, 3/12–3/20)	(graph, 4/1–4/10–4/20)	(graph, 5/10–6/10–7/10)	The defects include all those in the machining process, machine tools and jigs.
Machining time per item		(graph, 3/12–3/20)	(graph, 4/1–4/10–4/20)	(graph, 5/10–5/20–5/70)	Test-cutting time rose sharply due to increased rework.

Defects due to mechanical breakdown

Almost all defects due to mechanical breakdown originated in electrical systems, particularly since malfunctioning due to insulation failure results in all work being defective. Superiors were informed of these problems in order that the information could be passed on to the sections concerned and improvements implemented.

Deviations in castings

Deviations in castings appêared as tap breaking and dimensional defects. Information was passed on to the casting section and suggestions were invited for altering the method of manufacture and improving standards.

Changes in reference plane

Owing to changes in casting production methods, the reference plane was changed.

Deviations resulting from mistakes in installation

In order to eliminate individual variations in methods of hydraulic clamping of pallet tools, a mutual agreement was arrived at for establishment of operating standards, and points to be checked during mounting were determined. In addition, a group proposal was made for achieving uniformity in crankcase clamping and at the same time changing the balance of forces. More than ten other suggestions for improvement were made and adopted.

Summary of results

Owing to implementation of these various measures effected on the basis of considerable effort, it can be said that at present reasonably stable production is continuing. Results attained are shown in figure 4, but this shows only numerical results. There are many other results which are not tangible, in that through the medium of the meetings the operators have learned teamwork and have formed closer personal relations. It is unlikely that these results could have been achieved without the circle activities of data collection, brainstorming, and exchange of opinion. Of course, it is also true that acknowledgement is due to the guidance of superiors and the assistance of the men of related sections. At any rate, it was possible to advance to the collection of data for a third improvement programme.

Since the introduction of the transfer machine, the plans aimed at attaining full operation quickly have to some extent been realized. To obtain results exceeding those achieved so far, circle members and related personnel are taking advantage of the experience outlined above and are considering a third programme of improvement which we are starting to implement. It is expected that this will result in further improvement. In looking around us we find that there are still many problems in need of solution, and it is only by means of greater and greater encouragement of circle activities that we can discharge the responsibility that has been given us for increasing productivity in this day of continued technological innovation.

Case 12

Increasing efficiency by improving operation methods

Yasuyuki Yamazaki

This plant manufactures rubber belts for belt conveyor equipment. As can be seen in figure 1, these belts contain a core (consisting of cotton canvas, synthetic canvas, wire, steel bands, etc) that is rubber covered.

At present, the plant operates on a shift system, and circle activities are a part of the system. Our 12-man circle meets on Saturdays at intervals of every two weeks from 4 to 5 a.m. during the night shift. Written reports concerning the programme are distributed to the circles on other shifts; measures for improvement are studied and implemented on the basis of the minutes of circle meetings.

Case study: Increasing efficiency by improving operation methods

The production process
This shop is in charge of the conveyor belt form (see figure 2). Two canvases which were glued together using a calender roller in the previous process, are in the new process cut and then pressed by a forming machine to cover the belt with rubber before it is finished.

This plant manufactures rubber belts for belt conveyor equipment. As can be seen in figure 1, these belts contain a core (consisting of cotton canvas, synthetic canvas, wire, steel bands, etc) that is rubber covered.

Selecting this theme
According to the company's plan for 'Improving Forming and Vulcanization Efficiency' adopted in 1967, the theme 'Better Efficiency from Better Operation Methods' was taken up by the forming section.

* Yasuyuki Yamazaki is Forming Work Team Chief, First Production Section, Kobe Plant, Mitsuboshi Belt Co., Kobe

Figure 1 Cross-section, conveyor belt

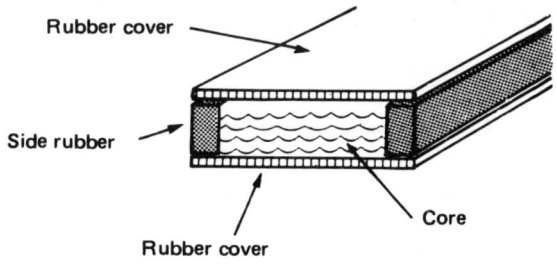

Figure 2 Conveyor belt manufacturing process

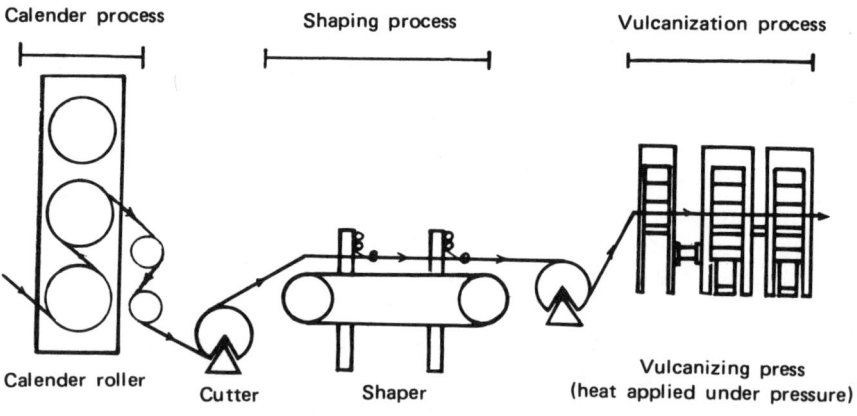

Our goal

Our goal was made to increase efficiency in forming 30 per cent by the end of March, 1968 (in the light of the long-term plan as well as by results achieved and by other goals established for the section). (In our company, the rate of work efficiency is calculated

INCEASING EFFICIENCY BY IMPROVING OPERATION METHODS

Figure 3 Weight of tasks in the forming process

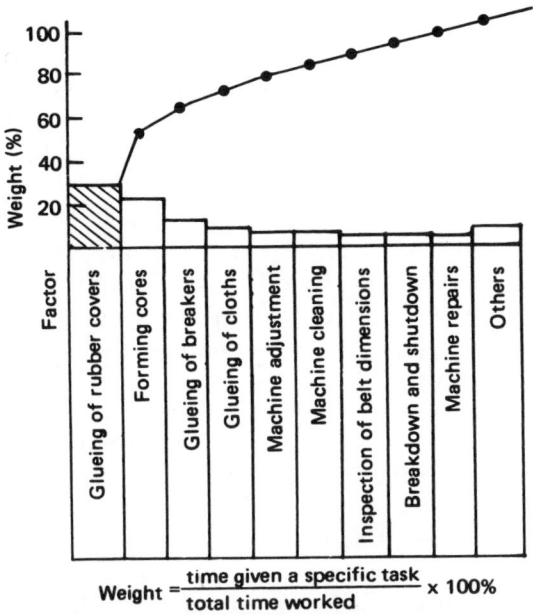

$$\text{Weight} = \frac{\text{time given a specific task}}{\text{total time worked}} \times 100\%$$

Figure 4 Weight of work involved in glueing rubber covers to belt cores

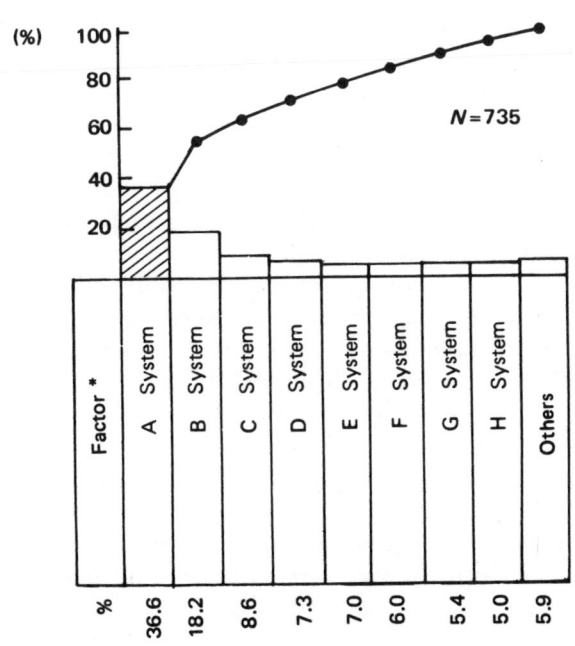

*Rubber cover type

by the standard cost accounting equation: Number of actual tasks involved in a process divided by the number of standard tasks in the same process times 100 per cent. All possible efforts are made to keep the number of actual tasks below the number of standard tasks and therefore the lower the rate below 100 per cent the better.)

Understanding and analyzing the present situation
A Pareto diagram was prepared for each task in the forming process and, as can be seen from figure 3, glueing rubber covers was found to be the most important task. This problem was then tackled. All members of the circle cooperated in preparing a cause and-effect diagram (figure 5) to improve the efficiency of the rubber cover operation.

As the main factors, equipment, methods, materials, and personnel allocation were taken up. With the forming machine used previously, glueing rubber covers involved more than one task (because the outer and inner surface covers were glued separately) except in special cases. Whether it would be possible to reduce the number of tasks to one was a key problem because operational efficiency could not otherwise be improved. First, it was decided to study the equipment. There were two types of forming machines in use: flat and circular.

By improving the equipment, there arose the possibility of changing the method. With both the flat and circular machines, it was possible to glue a rubber cover on one side at a time, but with the circular type machine it was also possible to glue covers to both sides at the same time.

It was suggested that the materials employed could be changed. A Pareto diagram for work involved in glueing each type of rubber cover rubber is wound. layers tend to stick together; therefore, from this diagram, type A requires most work. It was known previously that the same type of rubber was very adhesive because of its softness. When rubber of this type was rolled onto the winder, it was difficult to separate it from the liner cloth. (When the cover to belt cores was plotted as shown in figure 4. As is evident before forming it into a belt, a liner cloth, which does not stick to rubber, is placed between the layers.) This involved extra tasks and repairs.

In this connection an examination was made to determine whether all liner cloths in use were suitable. The belts requiring

IMPROVING OPERATION METHODS

Figure 5   Characteristic cause diagram

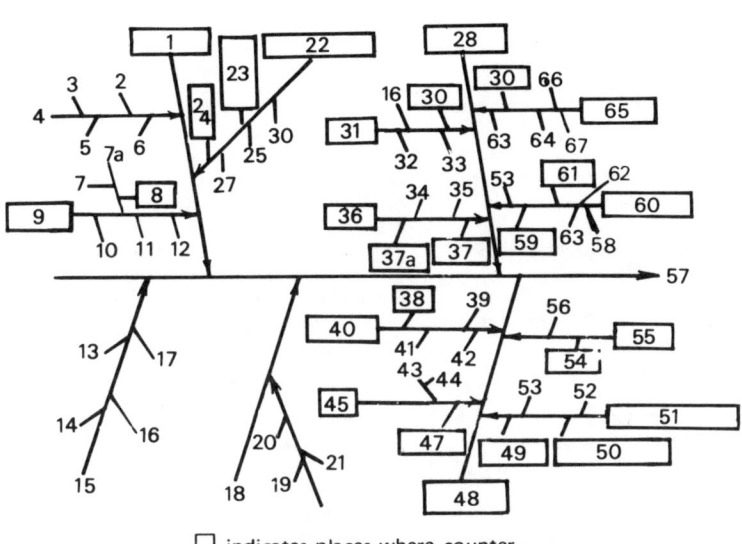

☐ indicates places where counter-measures are considered possible

1. Material
2. Width
3. Thickness
4. Side rubber (Mr G)
5. Thinness
6. Narrowness
7. Oil resistance
7a Synthetic
8. Heat resistance
9. Rubber composition (Mr E)
10. Bonding characteristics
11. Thickness
12. Natural rubber
13. Temperature and humidity
14. Walking space
15. Environment
16. Size
17. Lighting (Mr I)
18. Employees
19. Seniority
20. Training
21. Awareness
22. Liner cloth (Mr H)
23. Amount of wear
24. Length
25. Adequate
27 Width
28. Equipment
30. Inadequate
31. Roller (Mr C)
32. Height
33. Adequate
34. Manual operation
35. Adequate
36. Crane (Mr B)
37. Inadequate
37a Electrical operation
38. Thickness
39. External abnormality
40. Rolling thickness (Mr A)
41. Thinness
42. Inconsistency
43. Blade
44. Sharpness
45. Cutting (Mr J)
47. Cameron cutter
48. Method
49. Mechanical application
50. Simultaneous cover application
51. Rubber cover application (Mr D)
52. Single-side cover application
53. Manual application
54. Lift
55. Transport (Mr B)
56. Cog wheel
57. Improvement in efficiency of cover application process
58. Adequate
59. Automatic winding
60. Winders (Mr C)
61. Inadequate
62. Manual winding
63. Adequate
64. Size
65. Stand (Mr A)
66. Height
67. Inadequate

QUALITY CONTROL CIRCLE CASE STUDIES

Table 1

	Problems	Countermeasures
Equipment	Inadequate number of stands Inadequate number of liner cloth winders (for work in process) Inadequate number of lifting devices Inadequate number of liner cloth winders (for rolled rubber)	Installation of additional new winders and stands for the forming machines (by the construction, maintenance, and repairs section) Installation of new chain blocks (by the same section as above) Installation of additional liner cloth winders (by the same section as above)
Methods	Simultaneous glueing of rubber covers on both sides Thickness of rolled rubber covers Cutting of side rubber	With approval of the technical section, rubber was made to be rolled for all types of covers to the thickness as indicated to fit specific belts Cutting of the general-use rubber belts was assigned to the forming section. However, Long A-type cover belts, which require a long time for vulcanization, were to be made by having cutting performed by the shaping section while the rest of the cutting was performed during vulcanization
Materials	Quality of liner cloth (influencing whether rubber will stick to it, etc.) Length of liner cloth	A new liner cloth was used for A-type belts The length of the liner cloth used to roll the standard covering rubber was standardized at 200 m
		Administrative Compilation of essential points to check the general equipment Compilation of essential points to check the electrical equipment Preparation of a control chart for rubber covers thickness $(X-R)$ Compilation of maintenance points and water control points for the liners used with A-type belts

Table 2 Problem points and results of countermeasures

Problem points	Conditions	Countermeasures	Results
Rolled exterior of cover rubber	When the surface of the specified rubber is defective, air causes thickness defects	Control and standardization of the thickness of each of the various types of cover rubber	Surface defects caused by air eliminated by thickness still a problem
Hoists	Since lifting operations are performed with a chain hoist, the number of process steps, the danger involved, and the suspension position are inappropriate	Changing to an electric hoist and moving the centre of the I-beam	Lifting operations were speeded up and fatigue decreased
Cutting sides of cover rubber	Difficulties arise when cutting the upper and lower cover rubber by hand	Use of a Cameron cutter	It is necessary to restudy the problems of equipment location and zigzag movement of belts

Note: Information groups from the technical section of the plant are now studying the previous process steps and forming processes to solve the problem of cover rubber rolling. The engineering section and forming process people are studying problems relative to the cutting of the side cover rubber.

the A-type rubber cover, although consisting of fewer strips than any of the other belts, are mostly longer, and demand, and therefore production, are increasing.

To reduce the number of tasks in forming A-type rubber covers, measures were taken as follows to solve the problems of the equipment, methods and materials, as shown in table 1.

Backing paper was tested in connection with the adhesive properties of rubber, but the paper tore due to tension, and was marred by wrinkles. Therefore, it was impossible to use paper since the properties of the rubber cannot be altered.

Operations before and after improvements

Before the improvements were made, the cover rubber was applied to the under surface of the core from the winder by the No. 1 rollers, moved past the No. 2 rollers, and wound onto the final winder. The rubber was then applied to the other surface of the core in the same manner, which meant that application of the cover rubber to both sides of the core required two steps (see figure 6).

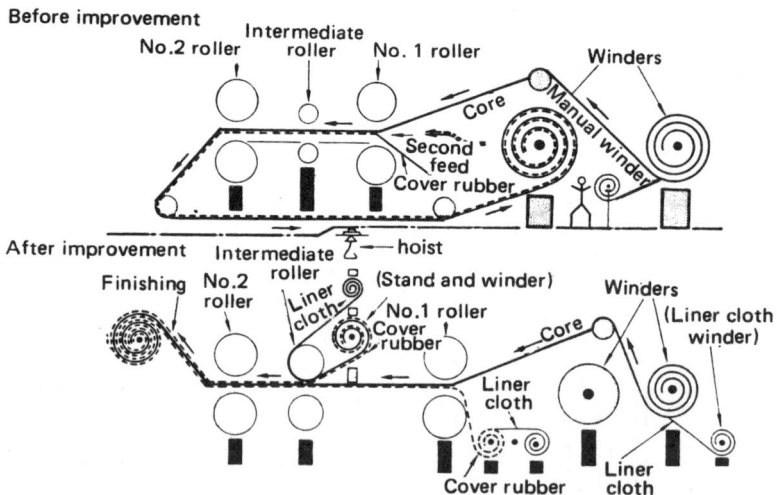

Figure 6 Rubber cover application process before and after improvements

In the improved process, the cover rubber is applied to the under surface of the core from the winder by the No. 1 rollers. The cover rubber for the upper surface is wound on a stand and winder located in front of the intermediate rollers, the liner cloth is removed by an intermediate roller, the roller, the rubber applied to the upper surface of the core, and the covered core then wound on the final winder. In this way, both surfaces of the core are covered simultaneously in a single step.

Before improvement, the liner cloth used on the winders was manually wound on a stand between the winders. After improvement, however, a special liner cloth winder was placed behind the final winder and winding performed automatically.

When this improved method was put into operation, the problems listed in table 2 arose and further countermeasures were required to solve them.

Effectiveness

The efficiency of the cover rubber application forming process, according to our calculation method (efficiency is expressed as a percentage of the standard; the lower percentage of standard the higher the efficiency) reached 44 per cent in March 1968, which meant a reduction of 56 per cent. The over-all forming process efficiency was reduced 32 per cent to 68 per cent (see figure 7).

Figure 7 Efficiency in conveyor belt shaping process (solid line) and efficiency of the rubber cover application process (broken line)

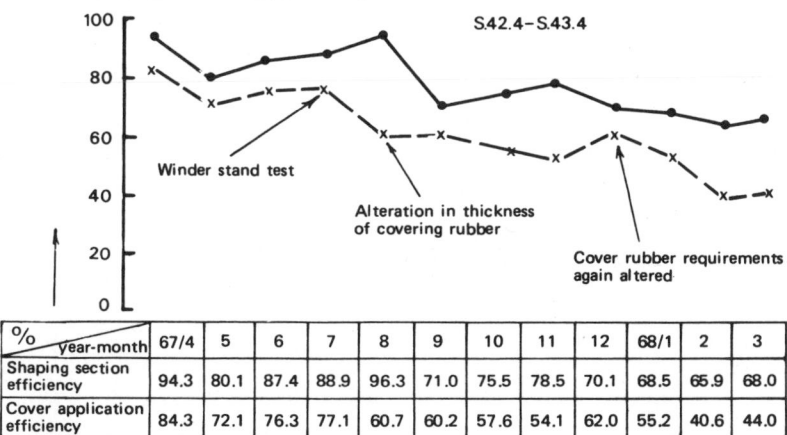

% year-month	67/4	5	6	7	8	9	10	11	12	68/1	2	3
Shaping section efficiency	94.3	80.1	87.4	88.9	96.3	71.0	75.5	78.5	70.1	68.5	65.9	68.0
Cover application efficiency	84.3	72.1	76.3	77.1	60.7	60.2	57.6	54.1	62.0	55.2	40.6	44.0

The original goal, a 30 per cent improvement in efficiency was attained in both cases.

With regard to economy, labor costs were reduced 2,100,000 yen (US$5,840) on a one-year basis (material, labour and other expenses necessary to make improvements cost 460,000 yen (US$1,280).)

Quality improvement was attained by removing one processing

step, leading to reduction of both inconsistencies due to elongation of intermediates and the need for repair work.

Since the use of liner cloth was made more efficient, the need for it decreased.

Standardization
Standard maximum thicknesses were determined for each type of cover rubber.

Concerning methods, standard belt and A-type shaping methods were standardized. Also, since the upper surface cover rubber is wound together with the liner cloth uniform winding is assured. Checking the provisions for intermediate dimensions have been altered (improvement of daily report).

Future problems.
1 Automation of side rubber cutting.
2 Reduction of surface defects and thickness inconsistencies in thick rubber covers.
3 Automation of side rubber application.
4 Re-examination of the use of backing paper.

Case 13

Improvement of the operating rate of synthetic yarn spinning

Nobuo Tetsu and Satoshi Kanei[*]

Management and history of our QC Circle activities

The QC Circle movement began in our company when a four-man secretariat established several QC Circles in the technical section of the manufacturing department. A leader was nominated for each group. Leader meetings are held to determine the "programme of the movement for the year" and how the movement would be managed. The programme is reviewed at the meeting of section chiefs, is included in the over-all factory policy, and is then announced throughout the factory.

The objectives of our circle activities are to promote the will to work, foster leadership among field supervisors, improve human relations, and increase worker morale.

Our QC Circle movement first gained momentum as an integral part of the quality control movement started in 1966 when a proposal to form QC Circles was proposed to the company improvement committee.

The circles born of this proposal consisted of a leader or supervisor, several foremen and production workers. Training of two participants in the movement as circle lecturers was completed in June, 1966, during which time QC Circles were established to investigate problems and make improvements. During this period, section and subsection chiefs gave their full support to create the most favourable atmosphere within each section.

In April and August, 1966, feeling that the time was ripe for the company to start its movement, we took part in inter-company symposia on the QC Circle movement, and the first QC Circle report meeting with Synthetic Yarn Subsection No. 1 (two reports

---

[*] Nobuo Tetsu is from the Technology Section, Production Department, and Satoshi Kanei is of No. 2 Section, Production Department, Toyo Chemical Co., Kamakura

QUALITY CONTROL CIRCLE CASE STUDIES

Figure 1 Pareto diagram for causes of production of grade B filament

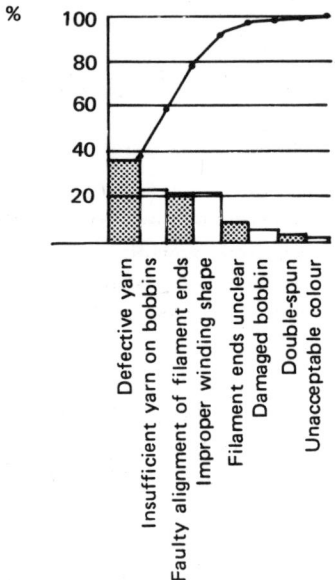

Figure 2 Pareto diagram for specific defects

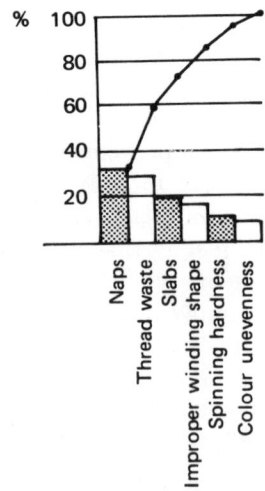

made) and Forming Subsection (one report made) was held in August. From 1967, with the intent of getting the ideals of the movement across to the workers, leadership was transferred from foremen to team captains. As of April, 1966, five intra-company report meetings had been held.

We intend to expand the QC Circle movement beyond our own production work to our subcontractors' factories.

Case study: Reduction in grade B filament yarn and improvement in the spinning operation rate

We manufacture fibres for Emvilon multi-filament, which is made into wigs, hair for dolls, and used in mats and carpets. The QC Circle movement ran into some difficulties when leadership responsibilities were transferred from foremen to team captains, who numbered from five to 10 and who had handled only general jobs. Neverethless, results were attained as presented below.

Reason for selecting the theme

The yield rate of Emvilon multi-filament was approximately 95 per cent. At the final selection for inspection, grade B filament yarn was detected, and the yield rate of first-grade filament yarn was 89 to 90 per cent. Because of this, reduction of the amount produced of grade B yarn was selected as the theme of our QC Circle movement. This theme was also selected to coincide with efforts to improve the operation rate from 89.4 per cent (for March, 1966 to February, 1967) to 92 per cent, which was the target percentage of the factory.

Cause-and-effect analysis of factors affecting grade B production of filament yarn

We spent two weeks analyzing the cause and effect of each factor affecting grade B filament yarn, and Pareto diagrams and a cause-and-effect diagram were plotted by all circle members (see figures 1 to 3).

Regarding the rate of operation, an analysis was made with a Pareto diagram for causes of downtime from March, 1966, to February, 1967 (see figure 4).

Further, the causes of trouble were investigated, and the downtime per failure for each machine for each cause, was calculated. (Downtime in one year due to shutdown totalled 5,225 hours.) The initial step, inspection for preventive maintenance, was made

OPERATING RATE OF SYNTHETIC YARN SPINNING

Figure 3 Toyo Chemical case study

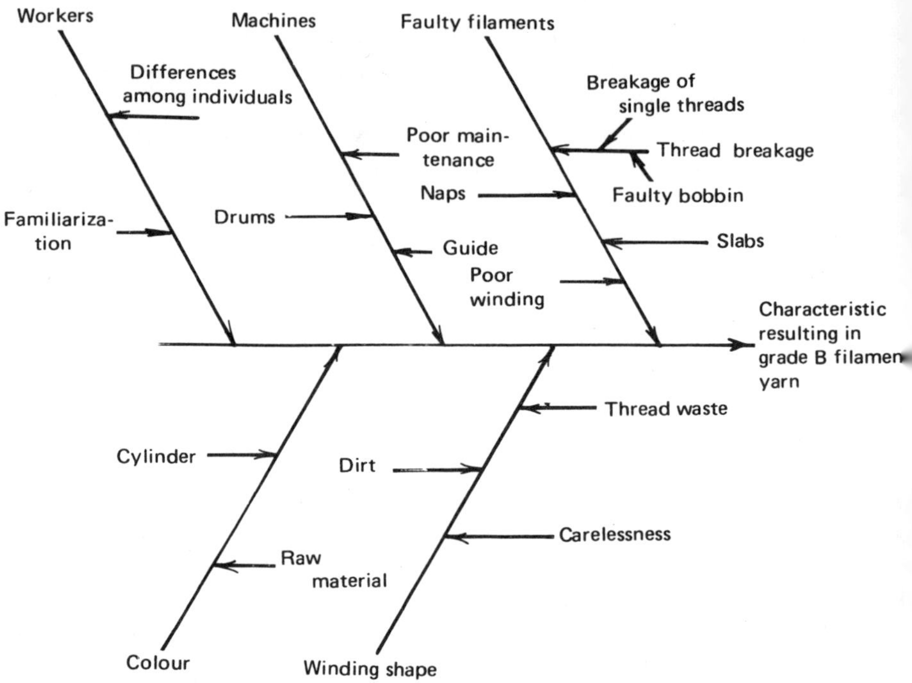

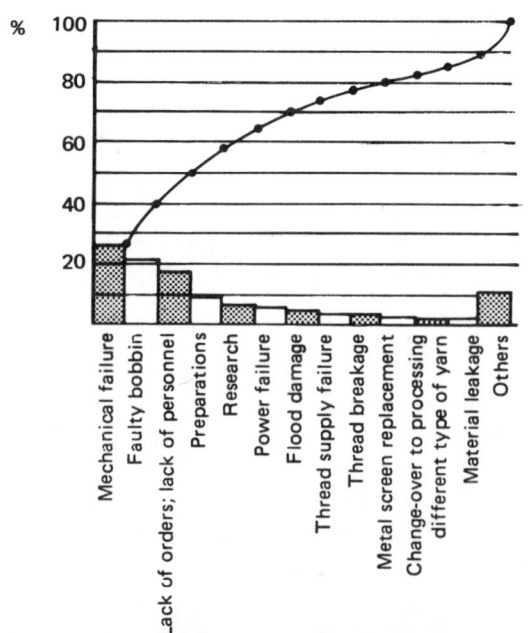

Figure 4 Pareto diagram for downtime

Note: Mechanical breakdown accounted for 25% of total downtime

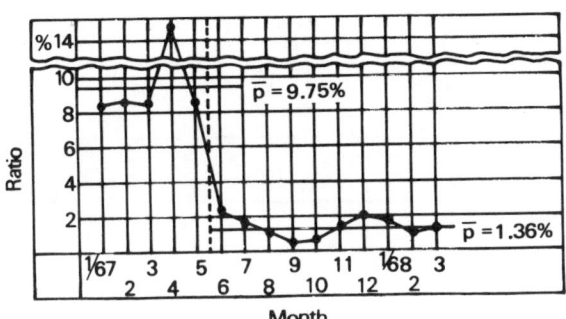

Figure 5 Yield ratio of grade B filament yarn

and spare parts were readied. Through these steps, troubles caused by failures of chains, thermostats, pins, etc were eliminated, resulting in a reduction of downtime by 1,062 hours on an annual basis.

Since only 0.6 improvement was attained through the foregoing step, further steps were taken. These are as in the following section.

Countermeasures
Spinning defects countermeasures: From results of a thread breakage inspection conducted for two weeks in January, 1967, it was ascertained that breakage was caused by stretching, filament breakage, and faulty winding of the main fibre. (In most cases, slabs* were found, and this indicates that the spinning process greatly affects all of the later steps in the process.) Therefore, first, to stabilize the spinning process, the proportions of materials with uneven scouring were kept to 7 per cent or below, in the mixing of fibres. Second, by improving the material supply system of the equipment, unevenness in supply was decreased so that yields before and after improvement could be compared and checked. Third, for test purposes, five machines were selected and operated for 10 days. The results are shown in table 1. From table 1, it was concluded that things were better after the improvement attempt and the above two countermeasures were put into effect.

Measures against machine breakdowns: An accident report form, to be delivered to the machine subsection, was drawn up. If a break-

---

* Slabs are bulges in the thickness of the yarn, usually with thin sections before and following the bulge. They create defects in cloth.

QUALITY CONTROL CIRCLE CASE STUDIES

Table 1 Results of test running five machines (unit: time available: %)

	Sample size	Mean value	Standard deviation (σ)	Test results
Before improvement	28	95.5	2.01	Difference is significant at the level.
After improvement	41	98.0	0.85	

Table 2 Machine breakdowns (unit: time in hours)

Period	Over-all downtime (A)	Monthly average	Number o. breakdowns (B)	(A)/(B)
March '66—Feb. '67	5225	470	6	72
Apr. '67—March '68	3107	258	6.7	38
Difference Time per breakdown	2118	212	0.7	34

down occurs it is reported immediately and repairs are made. Also, practice of daily checks with a check list has been in effect since June 1967, (every day, two workers complete this list for their machine) and if there is a breakdown, the check sheet is filled in as repairs are made. Further, in cooperation with the machine subsection, periodic lubrication and maintenance are carried out regularly by two workers.

Future plans include emphasizing that the workers must check their own machines and take responsibility themselves for the care of them, relying on the machine subsection only for the repair of parts which are liable to cause breakdowns.

Effectiveness of the QC Circle movement
Results are shown in table 2. By limiting the percentage of materials with uneven scouring and improving the supply method, the percentage of grade B yarn has been decreased. The countermeasures against machine breakdowns have resulted in a reduction of downtime. These results are evident from table 3 and figures 5 and 6.

IMPROVEMENT OF OPERATING RATE OF SYNTHETIC YARN SPINNING

Table 3 Effects of the QC Circle movement

Period	Percentage of grade B filament yarn	Period	Hours of machine down-time due to breakdowns	Hours of downtime due to other reasons	Operating ratio
Jan. – May '67	9.75%	March '66–Feb. '67	5225	21413	89.4%
June '67–March '68	1.36%	Apr. '67–March '68	3107	11716	94.0%
Difference	8.93%	Difference	2118	9697	4.6%

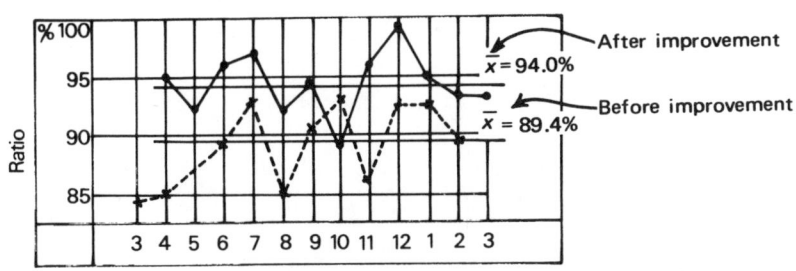

Figure 6 Operation ratio of spinning grade B filament yarn

1 With respect to downtime, the circle was almost entirely concerned with machine breakdown. However, the programme was doubly effective because of countermeasures to lower the percentage of grade B yarn and ways to improve the care taken by the workers. There was a difference in downtime of 45.2 per cent or 9,697 hours/year and an operating rate of 94 per cent, 2 per cent higher than the objective, was achieved.
2 A final calculation of the results shows that the reduction in grade B yarn has increased profits by 8.3 per cent (330,000 yen or US$917 a month) and down time is now only 808 hours a month, which means an additional profit of 257,000 yen (US$715) a month.

Standardization

As a result of reduction in the yield of grade B yarn, modifications made in each machine and the process alterations were added to the operation standards. The limits on the amount of materials with uneven scouring was discussed with the mixing subsection and process inspection standards and acceptance standards were determined. Measures against mechanical breakdowns were standardized and made known to all employees.

Case 14

Providing incentives to the QC Circle through an evaluation system

Tadao Koguri*

QC Circle activities in our company started in 1963. At the beginning, the movement was strong but after three to four years, workers began to merely go through the motions involved without any showing deep interest in the 'why' of circle activities, and the movement tended to stagnate. By investigating, we learned that the problem lay in the guidance and concern of the administrative supervisor who had been put in charge. As a countermeasure, we thought of introducing an individual evaluation system.

Our greatest return is that through this system we will effectively train 'people who get things done' and instill in them the will to challenge the future.

We introduced the individual evaluation system and overcame 'mannerizing' of the QC Circle activity. This was developed as a form of management by objectives. Examples of successes resulting from the introduction of the evaluation system are explained below:

To assure success of the departmental management policy of 1963, which aims at increasing quality consciousness, training was planned and carried out in cooperation with the personnel section, administrative division, which serves as the education centre for the entire company.

For teaching material we compiled our own texts, the first of which was entitled 'In Preparation for Pleasant Work Place and Pleasant Work.' There was a tremendous response and the education programme was therefore extended to include all production departments. As the outcome of this training, 'study groups' having the atmosphere of a discussion meeting centring around the first-line supervisors sprang up in every workshop.

---

* Tadao Koguri works in the Production Section, Main Plant, Suzuki Motor Co. Ltd., Hamana-gun, Shizuoka Prefecture.

This does not mean that there had been no opportunities in the past to plan meetings and faster development of skills, but the promotion of learning and awareness had never been the main subject. The study groups were then renamed 'QC Circles' and the programme began.

For management 'The Essence of Management' and 'Management Manual' were distributed to all circle leaders, and proved very helpful in our activities. All activities take place after working hours. Leaders collect the results in 'QC Circle study reports'. These results are reported to the promotion section of each department.

Circle leaders are selected by all circle members. The majority of them are squad or work team chiefs but circle leaders are not limited to group chiefs.

Introduction of the evaluation system

When looking for the reasons for stagnation of the circle movement, examination revealed that the major problems were that everything was being left up to the workers themselves, the guidance and concern of the control supervisors had deteriorated considerably, and the circle movement was not being viewed in the right way. In other words, adequate evaluation was not being carried out.

During company progress report meetings, reports were made but problems remained concealed as the power of expression was not adequate, although on the surface progress seemed to have been made. Conditions in some sections made it possible for a person's progress to be immediately evident, which was advantage, but in other sections in which direct observation was not possible, such an advantage did not exist.

The circle must generate its own driving force and therefore should have a high level of perseverence. Those having a sense of the future should want to participate in QC Circles. The money saved is naturally important but the endeavour should be even more important. It does not matter if you score a home-run; building up the score by a succession of hits is obviously important. With this understanding, in April, 1966, an evaluation score sheet was drawn up.

The importance of the evaluation points were first emphasized by the circles and a mood of 'Let's maintain the specifications, locate problems during work, and cooperate to eliminate problems' was created. Points which demanded consideration are described below.

Emphasis is on holding circle meetings
If we consider circle meetings from the two viewpoints of holding the meetings and members' attendance rates, holding the meetings is more important than the attendance rates. For example, holding circle meetings for QC Circles on shift duty is more difficult than holding meetings for circles on normal working hours. When holding meetings for circles on shift duty, that alone results in high evaluation and the score goes up considerably. Up to now, the evaluation sheet has been revised twice but the basic thinking has remained the same. Table 1 gives an example of the sheet in use at time of writing (i.e. autumn 1968).

The following may be used as an example. Regular-shift circle A with 12 members holds a 60-minute meeting with all members present. The score in this case is as follows: 10 points for one circle meeting and 5 points for attendance, which gives a total of 15 points. However, in circle B members of which also work on the regular shift, the 20 members had to do work on other shifts because of the nature of their work. One shift had 12 people and the other had eight. The shifts held meetings with full attendance. The score in this case was as follows: 20 points for two circle meetings, and a total of five points (2 + 3) for attendance. This makes a total of 25 points for circle B which is much higher than for circle A.

Demerits when production standards are not observed
Creation or revision of production standards results in a higher score but high quality can be assured by giving demerit points for nonconformity to standards. Previously, the promotion department (plant management staff in the engineering departments, etc.) conducted unannounced sampling checks in order to promote day-to-day control, but from June, 1967, the leaders and supervisory staff joined together to form a check group to promote conscientious work.

In connection with the leaders' training programme, leaders' study groups were established in October, 1966. As the company expanded, the circles increased and the number of new leaders outside the group chief class gradually increased. However, many of these

Table 1 QC circle evaluation sheet

						Section chief
		(Month)				
Section	Circle			Leader	Registered members	
Item	Evaluation item		Weight	Points	Remarks	

Item	Evaluation item		Weight	Points	Remarks			
Number of suggestions made	Number of improvements, ideas, opinions, and suggestions presented		2 x (cases)		Type of suggestion ( )		File number ( )	
	(Limited to QC Circle suggestions)							
Times Circle met	15 – 29 minutes		3 x (times)		(Date)	(Date)	(Date)	(Date)
	30 – 59 minutes		7 x (times)		"	"	"	"
	60 – 89 minutes		10 x (times)		"	"	"	"
	90 – minutes		13 x (times)		"	"	"	"
Attendance rate	– 59%		2 x (times)		"	"	"	"
	60 – 79%		3 x (times)		"	"	"	"
	80% –		5 x (times)		"	"	"	"
Money saved or suggestion rank	to 9,999 yen or 5th rank		10 x (cases)		Type of suggestion ( )	File Number ( )	Money saved or suggestion rank for one case a month	
	10,000– 49,999 yen or 4th rank		30 x (cases)		"	"		
	50,000– 99,999 yen or 3rd rank		70 x (cases)		"	"		
	100,000–199,999 yen or 2nd rank		100 x (cases)		"	"		
	200,000 yen or 1st rank		170 x (cases)		"	"		
SOS SIS	Correction of errors		1 x (cases)					
	Formulation, revision		5 x (cases)					
Report given at QC Circle conference			40 x (cases)		Conference name			
Report published in	QC magazine		40 x (cases)		Name of magazine, issue			
SOS, SIS Violation	Type of standard is correct but not conformed to		–15 x (cases)		One check in three months			
	Type of standard not correct and could not be conformed to		–10 x (cases)					
TOTAL								
Details of SOS, SIS	SOS, SIS Division	New standard no.	Entry error		Enforcement	Revision		

Note: 1. When the QC Circle meets, this list must be submitted before the 10th of the following month. (If it is not submitted, the circle meeting will not be recognized as such.)
2. For the money saved in (4), supporting material in written form must be submitted with this evaluation list (except for suggestions).

people did not receive leaders training and therefore such people were not very effective in taking direct action.

The study groups were planned to promote exchange of experiences and opinions to improve the calibre of the leaders. At first, lecture meetings with instructors invited from outside the company were held often. However, now that the level has been improved, the need for such meetings has decreased and they are held only about once every six months.

From stagnation to an effective movement

The evaluation sheets are filled out once a month and must be submitted by the seventh day of the following month. If a self-examination is made, the results of the self-examination are presented at the same time.

Generally, evaluations are determined without concern for related individuals, who only hear of the evaluation results. They have no idea about the process of evaluation. Therefore, while the next period goals may not be so well understood and there may be some distrust concerning superiors, the general feeling is that everyone just must somehow persevere. However, with the QC Circle evaluation, a score is obtained depending upon whether the movement is active or not and since self-evaluations are also submitted, such mistrust is completely eliminated.

Evaluation score will be high only if efforts are made and results produced; in this every worker is equal. It is considered that this feeling will result in amiable circle activities, and guidance has been given with this in mind.

As can be seen from the example of improvement suggestions shown in figure 1, the results have been very good. The company received the third FQC prize and the director's award from the Science and Technology Agency five times. Including the third QC Conference in 1964, 27 reports had been given by late 1968 at the main plant. These successes are the result of the ordinary endeavours of the supervisory staff. The results in the end are all based on mutual understanding and agreement.

The workers are now more conscious of quality and even when production standards are not posted, they can distinguish defective products and remove them. When faults are detected the worker responsible is not censured; the blame is placed on the cause. In

QUALITY CONTROL CIRCLE CASE STUDIES

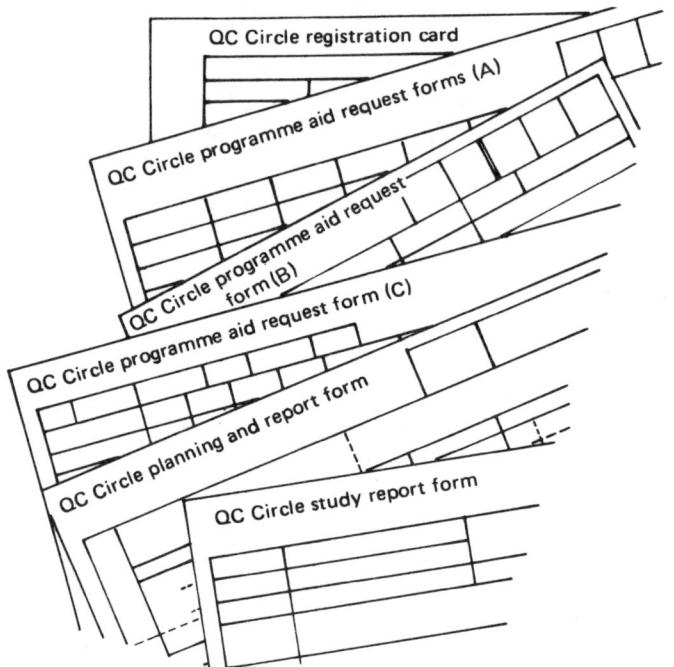

Figure 1 Main Forms Used by the QC Circle

this way, the workers are bettering themselves and the standards are being revised to be made more practical.

Every month the evaluation lists are totalled and the rankings plus a breakdown of the scores are returned to the leaders. From a careful consideration in the promotion department based on the totals for each period, the first awards are decided and 20 of the 54 circles receive prizes ranging from the president's prize to prizes for effort.

The president's prize is given for scores of 600 points and above. At present, however, to promote a balanced circle movement, four factors are required: a circle meeting score of 42 points or above, an attendance score of 10 points or above, money saved score of 10 points or above, and an over-all score of 180 points or above. These conditions must now be met for the prizes to be awarded.

The circles were not backward about receiving prizes. The feeling of perfection when difficult goals are achieved adds to self-confidence and gives a stimulus to other circles. Based on this experience, we have been able to train effectively 'people who get things done' and have created the will to challenge problems.

Case 15

Reduction in deflection of gear shafts
Gen Otsuki[*]

The Matsumoto factory, engaged in mass production of power meters and semi-conductor products, is paying special attention to improving management in the interest of conserving labour and elevating the control level in order to guarantee quality. For higher quality and greater productivity, it is believed necessary not only to use physical production technology but also to apply managerial techniques based on industrial psychology and use scientific management techniques as effectively as possible.

In view of this, QC Circles were established at the factory in November, 1966, the 'Quality Control Month' designated by JUSE. Thus, the start of the QC Circle movement at the factory was late as compared to that of other organizations because at first we feared that to start too suddenly would not help attain our objectives and that circles would not last long. Because of this, we allowed a preparatory period to lapse, during which an atmosphere for such a movement was fostered. Quality systems tables were prepared and problems were located. Themes and target figures were determined through discussions. After this lead period, the QC Circles were inaugurated. Although the circles are still young, improvements are briskly suggested, human relations in the circles have improved, and the workers have come to know the true importance of quality, process, and cost.

Typical case studies of QC Circle management
Number of QC Circles
At present, 165 circles are registered in the production divisions, and 37 circles in non-production divisions. The circle leaders were selected independently, and among them are a number of women.

---
[*] Gen Otsuki is from the Work Study Section, Fuji Electric Co., Matsumoto factory, Matsumoto City

QUALITY CONTROL CIRCLE CASE STUDIES

Activities and follow-up action

Once a month, reports are submitted through the chiefs in direct command of the circles to the committee for promotion of the QC Circle movement, these reports are used as material for ascertaining the progress of the movement and means of its promotion.

The circle leaders within each subsection meet once a month to discuss their activities for mutual enlightenment and improvement through suggestions and follow-up action.

Since there is a large number of circles, subcommittees of circle leaders, organized on the basis of either specific machines (in production divisions) or individual sections (in non-production divisions), meet every other month for discussions.

At the annual exchange-of-experience conference of the QC Circles in the factory, attended by superintendents and section chiefs, case studies are announced by circle leaders.

To promote the QC Circle movement, training is given, the morning shop assembly is used to advantage, and leaflets are distributed. One method we use is called the 'QC control panel' (see figure 1), which is posted conspicuously to catch the eyes of the circle members. The outer ring stands for QC, and the inner ring for safety. When the target for a month (each month is represented by the numerals 1 to 12) is reached, they are coloured blue. If the target is not attained, they are coloured red.

Figure 1 QC control panel

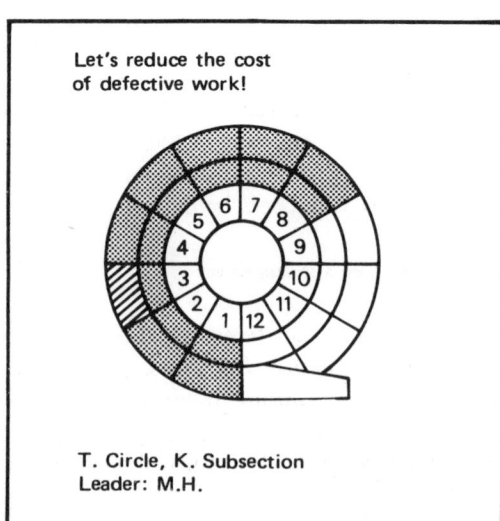

Case study: Reduction in deflection of gear shafts

Circle's goal and activities

The 16-member Aoki circle belongs to a subsection which assembles electrical meters and devotes itself to the assembly of gear mechanisms. The target was to reduce deflection of gear shafts to less than 0.6 per cent.

The subsection has 200 workers, more than 80 per cent of whom are women. This kept the circle activity low. In view of this, June 1968 was set aside as 'QC Month' for this subsection, and circle activities were encouraged by distributing leaflets and by taking advantage of the morning shop assemblies and leaders' meetings.

When this case study was written, the assembly subsection was trying to establish rules of circle activities. A leaders' meeting is held on the 15th of every month, reports are submitted on the 25th of each month, and morning QC shop assemblies are held twice a week. Thus, the causes of defects are being analyzed and circle activities are being promoted.

Through the above activities, an atmosphere has been fostered in which reports and discussions are made before trouble appears instead of the workers taking action only after being told to do so.

Reason for adopting the theme

The Aoki circle is in charge of assembling gears mainly by press-fitting shafts into gears. Because the cost of deflection in gear shafts accounted for about 40 per cent of the cost of all defective work in assembling gears, and also in view of the cost reduction goal of the subsection, it was decided to make the target reduction of defects 50 per cent.

Analysis of causes of deflection

It was revealed that the actual rate of deflection in gear shafts was 1.2 per cent. To determine the causes, a cause-and-effect diagram was prepared and analysis was made by all circle members. As a result, it was revealed that the major causes were centring of the holder, curvature of the shaft, and eccentricity of the boss.

Corrective measures

Centring of the holder: If the shaft is misaligned in the gear when press-fitted, the holder is scored and centring is affected. To guard against this, instruction was given to check the holder after misalignment had occurred.

Figure 2 Holder, before and after improvement

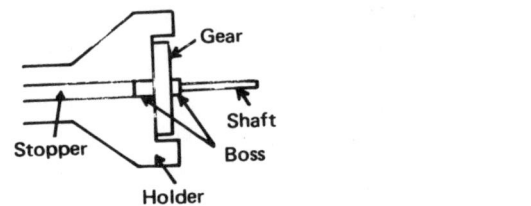

Before improvement   After improvement

Curvature of the shaft: In the previous process the shaft underwent polishing trommel in a barrel. Since it was discovered that warping occurred during this process, the fill rate of polishing material was changed from 50 per cent to 70 per cent of the volume of the barrel and the rate of rejections caused by warping was lowered.

The material for the shaft had been processed in the order of polishing — degreasing — pressure fitting. It was discovered that the warping was caused by transportation and loading/unloading for the cleaning process; after discussion this process was eliminated.

Eccentricity of bosses: Insertion by force hitherto had been carried out by receiving the boss with the stopper. Due to a wide variation in the length of the bosses, the gear surface positions gave rise to bending in accordance with the amount of floating of the bosses. The final result was gear misalignment.

In the improved method, the shape of the holder was changed from an over-all side surface to a partial plane meeting the outer peripheries of the gear, and the support of the gear was positioned away from the centre so that permanent deformation of the gear would not occur even if the stopper were floated by the shortest boss (due to non-uniformity of over-all boss length) or if the gear were warped (see figure 2).

Results

From the initial 1.8 per cent, the rejection rate has been reduced gradually each month until a percentage below the target figure of 0.6 per cent was obtained in less than five months.

Case study: Reduction in defect rate of small electrical component assembly

The circle and their goal

The 13-girl 'Ea' circle handles small electrical assemblies. Their target was reduction of the rejection ratio from 1.8 per cent to 0.9 per cent.

This group had formerly overlooked methods which were recommended to it. The attitude of those receiving advice led to deterioration of attitude of those giving advice.

After QC activities were started, however, attitudes changed; advice was freely given and willingly accepted. Now, with active attitudes prevalent, proposals for improvements flood each meeting, and foremen are overwhelmed with the degree of happiness shown by these ladies as they go about their work.

As circle activities have become brisk, they bring effects which are felt at all phases. In 1967, the rectifier group of the Ea Circle was cited for its excellent proposals for improvements and new contributions. The citation was awarded for excellence also from the standpoint of safety, defect reduction and yield increase.

Activities of the 'Ea' circles were fruitful because an area of responsibility had been assigned to each member in taking data, preparing graphs, and handling meetings.

Reason for taking up the theme

Small electrical products are assembled by conveyor lines, on which as many as 300 types of products are handled. Moreover, delivery terms are comparatively short. Due to these factors, faulty assemblies were often found. A target figure for defect reduction for 1968 was made the management policy of the factory. The aim of the circle was to reduce defects by half.

Investigation

In analyzing past data on defects it was revealed that the defect ratio was 1.8 per cent of all assembled products. Investigation was made into causes of defects, employing cause-and-effect diagrams and Pareto diagrams, and brainstorming took place with all members participating. Through this investigation, it was revealed that the major causes were faulty operation on the part of individual workers, installation of wrong parts, and shifts in amounting angles resulting from amounting bolts.

Corrective measures

Faulty operation on the part of individual workers: The number of rejects and the reasons for rejection were fed back rapidly from the assembly line inspector to the concerned workers, in order to instill in them a sense of responsibility.

Installing the wrong parts in the wrong model units: Stored parts were clearly identified. Gauges were provided for boxes of parts of the same shape but different thickness, and the thickness was checked before dispersing parts.

Shifts in angle caused in amounting bolt: The operations performed by this section was such that products of dozens of different models are alternately assembled daily according to order. The height of the bolt clamping tools was adjusted for individual cases. As a countermeasure, patterns for the flow of products each day were established so that the height adjustment of clamping tools could be substantially simplified.

Results

From the initial 1.8 per cent defect rate, rejections were reduced to 0.6 per cent in six months.

In the above, I have outlined and exemplified QC Circle activities at the Taga Factory. Recently, circle activities have shown their full worth in routine factory operations. On the other hand, the activities of some circles appear dull and stereotyped. We intend to provide stimulation periodically to revitalize the circle movement with the ultimate objective of developing circle activities from passive 'obedient movements' into active 'spontaneous movements.'

Case 16

Improvement in cylinder bore smoothness

Jiro Takeda*

Before training personnel for industry, it is first necessary to establish a systematic basis upon which employee initiative can be promoted. In our plant, a training system was established after investigating and consolidating all of the training methods previously used. In other words, to make training effective we devised a plan and then systematized it. Thus, the required training is introduced in a constructive way, the necessary elements are included, and any defects are ironed out as the system develops.

One aspect of this system is the establishment of self-improvement groups. The aims and the means of introducing and managing QC groups were publicized and representatives were sent to regional QC group conferences and other QC activities. Employees were expected to form circles on their own initiative.

During the second half of 1967, this part of the plan gained momentum and in November, nine groups with a total of 88 members were established. Since then, the number of circles has gradually increased and the movement is going strong.

Aim of the QC Circle movement

Fuji Heavy Industries produces a wide range of products, such as automobiles, buses, airplanes and rolling stock, and the company's factories manufacture small motors for general use, agricultural equipment, automobile parts, etc. A main product is the general purpose engine known by the brand name 'Robin.'

More than ten basic models of the engine with cylinder displacements ranging between 70cc and 800cc are in production, with many specifications established as they are used as agricultural

---

* Jiro Takeda is Chief, Quality Control Department, Omiya Plant, Fuji Heavy Industries, Ltd., Omiya City, Saitama Prefecture

equipment, generators, pumps, construction equipment, etc. Therefore a system is required which will prevent oversights in quality supervision, manufacturing methods and techniques, etc. This means that a well-organized QC movement is required on the shop floor.

Aims of promoting the QC Circle movement, which consist primarily of developing employee skill and ability are as follows.

Effective use of knowledge and ability
The average years of service of employees is long and therefore there are many who have a considerable amount of knowledge and ability. This store of knowledge and ability can be used effectively in producing quality in products.

Elimination of defects caused by carelessness
We must look at our products from the viewpoint of the customer. When many different types of products are made, defects caused by carelessness will be eliminated and product quality guaranteed if we look at them in this way.

Encouragement of an active dialogue between the foreman and his men
Workers have few chances to leave their machines and speak with the foreman. But through participation in QC activities of all shop personnel under the leadership of the foreman, an active dialogue between them can be encouraged for better human relations.

Present state of the movement

Matters are left to the leaders of each circle, but advice and cooperation are given by supervisors and quality control inspection, and engineering sections as necessary.

Circle methods: The circle members report problems to the leader who assesses their importance and influence, selects a thematic problem, and formulates a proposal containing the reason for selection of the problem, the aim of the improvement, the appraisal of its effects (cost-wise as far as possible), the steps to be taken, personnel and time required in making the improvement. After being checked by the team leader and supervisor concerned with the circle, the proposal is submitted to the head of the section and the QC department.

Circle activities: Small groups formed within the circle often discuss means of handling problems, making improvements, and other matters. These discussions usually take place during the lunch hour. With the approval of the section chief, they may take place within working hours but each meeting is limited to 30 minutes. The entire circle meets once or twice a month after working hours. During these meetings opinions are exchanged on proposals to be implemented, and progress of proposals being implemented is discussed. A combined check is also made by circles concerning certain problems.

Action after the improvement has been made: The circle leader draws up a report concerning the improvement. This report contains factor-wise causes of the problem, the actual steps taken in solving it, names of those who took charge of the task, the time taken, the effects appraised, and adoption of a standard and other results produced (in an estimated amount of money saved or in the number of jobs reduced) and follow-up measures.

Copies of this report are circulated to the chief of the section concerned, the product control department, and the subsection chiefs for reference.

Effectiveness of the Circle and future plans

The results so far indicate that the number of improvements and group suggestions will increase from now on. This will contribute to better products and lower costs. In shops where work is likely to be routine, the effectiveness of the QC circles is obvious because of the results in terms of self and mutual development. Within one year the results of the programme are being felt all over the plant.

Case study: Improvement of cylinder bore smoothness

This shop, No. 2 Mechanical Subsection of No. 2 Machine Section consists of a supervisor (subsection chief) and 48 men working under him. It produces crankcases, connecting rods, camshafts, crankshafts, etc. for the general-purpose engine. There are eight QC Circles headed by junior team leaders in this shop.

The improvement of the smoothness when machining cylinder bores as devised in this shop is introduced below.

Reasons for taking up this problem

When conducting finish boring of cylinders (hereafter referred to as FB), rough spots may be produced, which are major defects.

QUALITY CONTROL CIRCLE CASE STUDIES

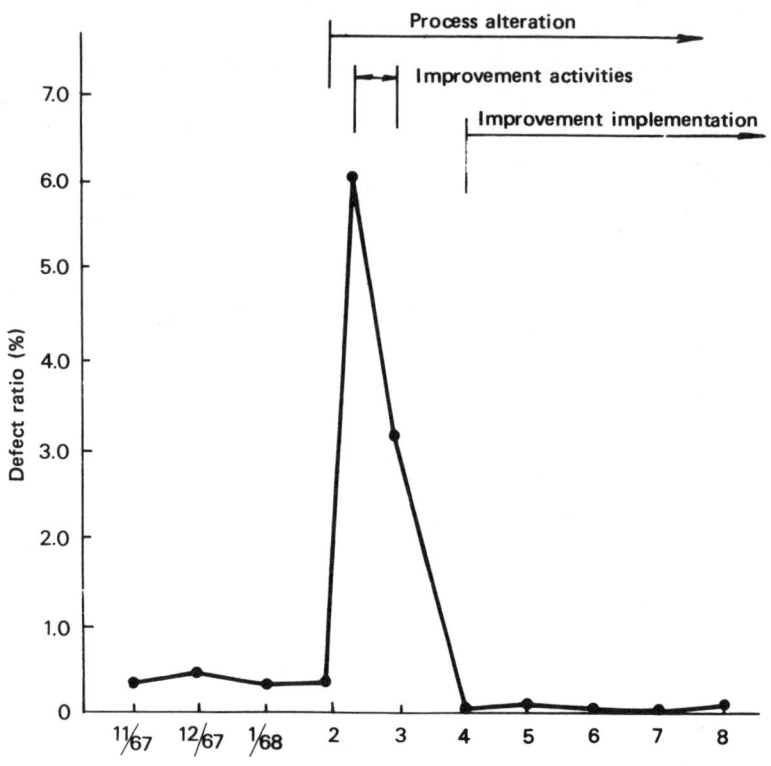

Figure 1 Defect ratios before and after process improvement

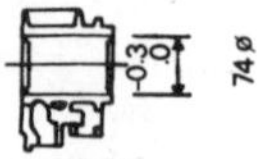

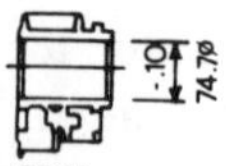

Figure 2 Change in the process

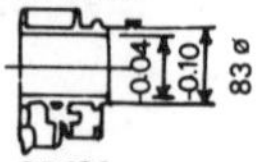

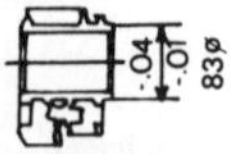

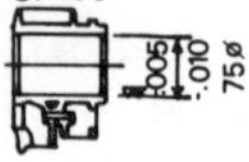

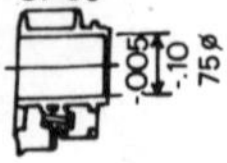

IMPROVEMENT IN CYLINDER BORE SMOOTHNESS

The QC group in the section in question took up this problem.
The defect ratio before and after the process change and improvement are shown graphically in figure 1.

Changes in the process
Alterations in the process were made by abolishing machining step number 20 and developing a newly-designed FB processing jig, using two fittings instead of one. Also, hydraulic clamping of the part was adopted instead of manual clamping (see figure 2).

Analysis of causes and comparison of before/after conditions
All data concerned with defect causes, with special emphasis on those related to process changes, were represented in a cause-and-effect diagram and investigated (see figure 3). When each cause was investigated separately (see table 1), it was found that the clamping method was the principal cause of defects.

In relation to clamping methods, the former method made use of only one fitting. The external diameter of the cylinder skirt was 83 mm $^{-0.04}_{-0.10}$ and the internal diameter of the pilot bushing on the jig was 83 mm -0.05, so that was 0.90-0.15 mm play. Also, in the old clamping method, clamping plates were fastened by means of hand-tightened bolts (see figure 4). When positioning the cylinder to the tool, the operator used one hand to hold the

Figure 3 Cause-and-effect diagram

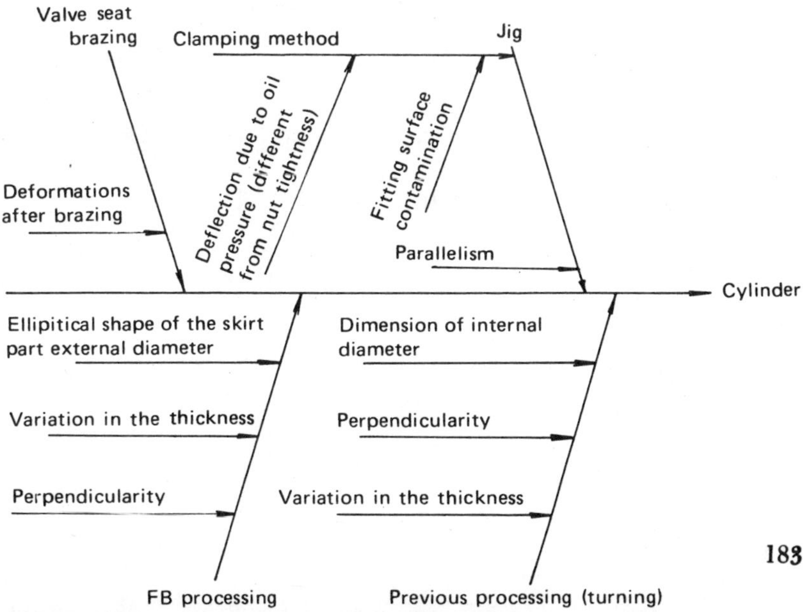

QUALITY CONTROL CIRCLE CASE STUDIES

Table 1 Investigation of specific causes

Main cause	Result of investigation

1 Jig or clamping method
   Contamination on the fitting surface
   Deflection due to oil pressure
   (different from manual method)
   Parallelism of the jig
	No problem
	Problematic
	
	No problem

2 Prior processing
   Internal diameter dimensions
   Internal diameter perpendicular with respect
   to the fitting surface
   Discrepancies in thickness of the skirt part
	No problem
	
	No problem
	Slightly problematic

3 FB processing
   Elliptical shape of the external diameter of
   the skirt part
   Discrepancies in the thickness
   Internal diameter perpendicular with respect
   to the fitting surface
	
	No problem
	No problem
	
	No problem

4 Brazing valve seat Deformation after brazing	No problem

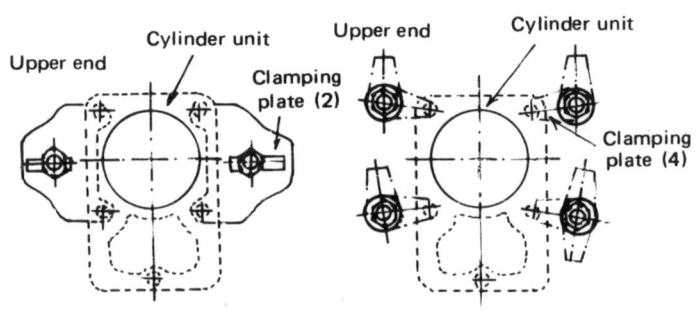

Figure 4 Clamping method

Old clamping method (manual method)　　　New clamping method (oil pressure)

cylinder, and the cylinder was positioned by the lower end, using the force of the weight of the cylinder. The cutting tool initially was placed, generally, at the lower end of the cylinder's internal diameter.

The new clamping method utilizes two fittings instead of one, and the dimensions of the cylinder skirt external diameter and the pilot bushing's internal diameter were left as before. Clamping plates, however, were fixed to the cylinder at an angle of about 90 degrees from the upper end.

When fixing the cylinder to the jig, the operator removes his hands and operates the hydraulic lever. The four clamping plates should be moved at the same time, but if they are moved individually for some reason, the cylinder is pushed in the direction opposite to that of the clamping plate that was tightened first. Therefore, the direction in which the cylinder is pushed varies according to the sequence in which the clamping plates are tightened.

The cutting tool was started, as in previous practice, at the lower end of the cylinder internal diameter.

Causes of defects
The following were identified as causes of defects:

The play between the external diameter of the cylinder skirt and the internal diameter of the processing-tool-positioning bushing was too great.

The cylinder is pushed obliquely upwards according to the tightening sequence of the clamping plates. However, the cutting bit is placed towards the lower end so that the amount of deflection is not uniform and in some cases, rough spots result.

Countermeasures, aims and procedure
Improvement of jig: The internal diameter of the bushing which positions the processing tool is decreased by 0.05 mm to become less than 83 mm then the play between the bushing and the external diameter of the cylinder skirt part becomes 0.04 to 0.10 (see figure 5).

After the cylinder is placed in the jig, the offset direction must be held constant and therefore the cylinder is pressed down at the lower end with the free hand during hydraulic clamping. In this way, proper tightening is possible even when the clamping plates are not tightened simultaneously.

Figure 5 Dimensions of fitting part of the improved tool

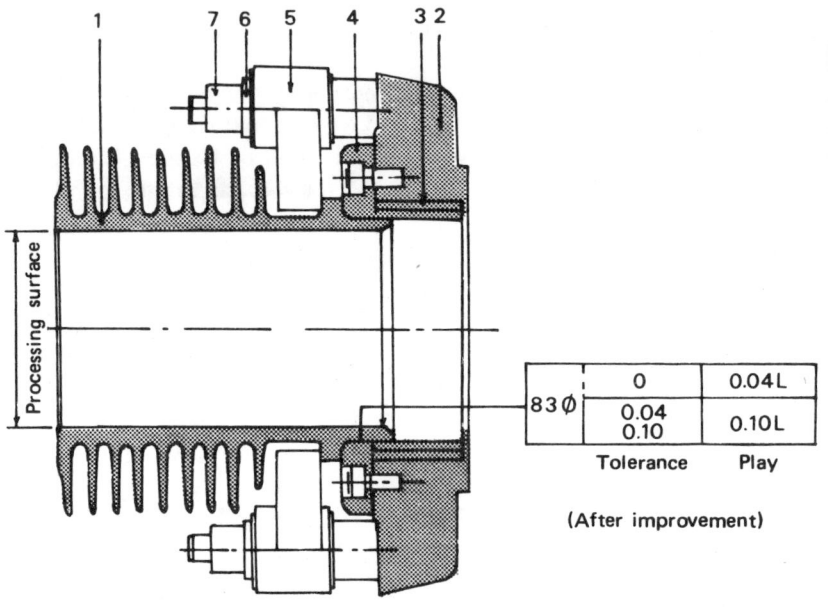

83⌀	0	0.04L
	0.04 0.10	0.10L
	Tolerance	Play

(After improvement)

1. Cylinder unit
2. Processing tool (unit)
3. Processing tool (stationary bushing)
4. Processing tool (positioning bushing)
5. Processing tool (clamping plate with guide)
6. Processing tool (rotating tightening shaft)
7. Processing tool (valve seat hexagonal nut)

Results of countermeasures

After the above-mentioned countermeasures were put into effect, defects due to roughness were completely eliminated and this clamping method was thus incorporated in the manufacturing specifications.

After this, the defect ratio became almost constant as can be seen from figure 1.

If we consider the above activities as merely resulting from the fact that the cylinder offset direction could not be held constant because of the excessive play between the cylinder skirt external diameter and the internal diameter of the positioning bushing of the jig, then the matter seems to be a rather minor one. Nevertheless, this seemingly insignificant fault had caused a considerable increase in product defects as well as a considerable processing loss. Therefore, this QC Circle project has proven itself highly effective.

Case 17

The QC Circle movement applied to shop requirements

Toshiharu Yokosawa[*]

This company was established after the war and therefore has only a brief history. A wide range of products are manufactured including music boxes, time switches, micromotors, industrial machinery, 8 mm cameras, tape recorders, etc. In 1962, the company was divided into four departments: music-box department, electrical department, machinery department, and optical department. Other company divisions include the head office, research department, and sales department. There are approximately 3,000 employees.

From 1963, basic training mainly in statistical quality control has been conducted by the company-wide Quality Control Committee (QCC). In March, 1965, the QCC held a second conference where case studies were reported (this later developed into the company's QC Circle conference). At that conference, circles were formed from those present and each circle was given the name of the group leader. These circles were registered with the Union of Japanese Scientists and Engineers and the QC Circle movement officially began in the shops with both circle and group activities. The movement gradually gained momentum (see table 1).

QC qualification
Training
The general conditions concerning the company's QC Circle movement have been described above. The movement has expanded greatly in the last two or three years, for reasons including implementation of the 'QC qualification' training system which is the company's special off-the-job training.

---

[*] Toshiharu Yokosawa is staff member, QC Circle Office and Chief, Production Engineering Section, Sankyo Seiki Manufacturing Co., Ltd., Suwa-gun, Nagano Prefecture.

QUALITY CONTROL CIRCLE CASE STUDIES

Table 1 Introduction and progress of the QC Circle movement in Sankyo Seiki

	1964	1965	1966	1967	1968
Formation	Quality control study meeting	Quality control committee →	Sectional meetings organized →		
Number of circles (yearly total)		35 circles	66 circles	95 circles	120 circles
Number of case studies reported (annual count)	14 cases (mainly staff and office organization)	1st half 9 cases / 2nd half 33 cases	1st half 66 cases / 2nd half 109 cases General employees	1st half 119 cases / 2nd half 155 cases Women employees	1st half 243 cases Women staff, women employees
Training		QC qualification system formed (A course) for top ranking supervisor class No. 1 line group leader staff	A course Squad chiefs	A course Squad chief, women B course Technical, management staff	
Number of QC Circle members (total)		1st period 17 / 2nd period 34	3rd period 68 / 4th period 118	5th period 144 / 6th period 172	7th period ?
Other activities		0/10 defect movement. Z movement	ZD movement. Management by results	ZD movement Management by results NE (no-error) movement	
Outside activities (exchanges)		QC teams sent outside company	All-Japan conference Kanto regional meeting Tokyo ZD study group meeting	QC, ZD exchanges	Nagano QC conference First National ZD conference

The original product made by this company is music boxes, but recently the production range increased so much that it became necessary to re-examine quality control procedures. In order to successfully compete with rival companies, a scientifically oriented QC programme is required which makes free use of various control systems based on a high level of original technology. Therefore, it is essential to train production-centre personnel in the constructive utilization of new techniques and equipment. The level of first-line supervisors holding the key to all shop processes was very low and therefore committee members investigated QC training for first-line workers and group leaders. The development of the QC qualification training system is explained below.

Basic conditions at the start of training
Various types of training had been previously conducted but it cannot be said that any of this training was really effective. Therefore, the aims and basic position were made absolutely clear before the training was started.

The training is carried out strictly for self-betterment and participation is purely voluntary. However, if the quality of future work does not improve because this knowledge is lacking, this is not the fault of the company. The company wants only those who feel that they are doing it for themselves and are thus highly motivated, to receive this training.

Textbooks and instructors are provided by the Quality Control Committee and therefore the students need only have the necessary time. Because activities are voluntary, no overtime pay is provided.

Employees who wish to be recognized as QC Circle participants must meet the conditions mentioned below.

The person must attain a score of 85 on a QC test.
All homework assignments must be submitted.
Personal experience must be reported.
A score of 85 must be attained on a general test.
The employee's attendance record must be over 95 per cent.
Employees who receive QC qualification must form QC Circles, act as circle leaders, and work towards factory improvement.

Further, five persons from each department will receive the training, making a total of 25 participants per class. In all cases, recommendation by the department chief is necessary. Training sessions are scheduled to meet every Thursday from 5.30 to 8.00 p.m. over a period of six months.

On the basis of the above, the programme began in 1965 and by late 1968, 160 persons had successfully completed the courses. In the beginning, only the A course was given but now there are two courses. The second, or B course, is especially for staff members and is intended to elevate staff training as the QC movement progresses (see tables 2 and 3).

Instructors are members of the QCC and are also usually specialists in staff and office organization. The aim is to bring the instructors and students as close together as possible during the course.

However, there is absolutely no relation between the QC qualification and positions or advancement in the company. Those who have the QC qualification receive no special considerations from the company and their salary is in no way affected. Nevertheless,

Table 2 Schedule, A course of QC training

No.	Type	Contents
1	Special lecture	QC is a guarantee of quality (Sect. 1 and 5)
2	Statistical method	Statistical thinking and methods
3	''	''
4	''	''
5	''	''
6		Experience reports (progress check)
7		'' ''
8		Statistical thinking and methods
9		''
10		Seminar, intermediate test
11	Special lecture	ZD essentials
12	''	Grasping problem points and making process improvements (Sect. 4)
13	''	Promoting the QC circle
14	''	Standardizing processes and methods (Sect. 3)
15	Control charts	Control chart considerations and methods
16		'' ''
17		'' ''
18	Sampling	Sampling considerations and methods
19		''
20		Intermediate test
21	IE	IE (work sampling: MTM)
22	''	''
23	Case reports	Case reports and investigations
24		''
25	Special lecture	Quality control promotion
26		Test

Table 3 Schedule, B course of QC training

No.	Type	Contents
1	Distribution	Population and samples
2		Regular hypergeometric series, Poisson distribution
3		Statistical variable distribution
4	Investigation of continuous data Deductions	Investigation and deduction sequences
5		Investigation of differences in population mean of variance, deductions, power of test
6	Investigation of enumerated data Deductions	Investigation of population fraction defective, deductions
7		Sample analysis method
8	First seminar	
9	Test (1)	
10	Control chart method	How to make control charts
11		Reading and efficiency
12		Reading and efficiency
13	Sampling inspection	Attribute sampling according to Japan Industrial Standards
14		OC curves MIL-STD
15		Variable sampling according to JIS
16	Correslation and regression	Investigation of correlation, deduction
17		Use of regression
18	Second seminar	
19	Test (2)	
20	Special lecture	How to further quality control
21	Special lecture	
22	Variance analysis	Considerations of variance analysis
23		One-way layout, two-way layout, and three-way layout methods
24		Models and unbiased estimator of population variance
25	Variance analysis	Models and unbiased estimator of population variance
26		Analysis of random models
27		Requirements for orthogonal polynomials (orthogonal analysis)
28	Third seminar	
29	Test (3)	
30	Sampling method	Random stratified sampling
31		Two-level and cluster sampling
32	Statistical experiment design method	Considerations concerning the experiment design method
33		Contingency tables
34		Contingency tables
35		Latin square
36		Latin square
37		Confounding method, etc.
38		Orthogonal array (experiment design)
39		Orthogonal array (experiment design)
40	Fourth seminar	
41	Test (4)	

the QC qualification is tending to become a general goal among the employees, many of whom do not want to be referred to as 'that guy without a QC qualification.' In spite of the rigorous conditions, the number applying for training has increased year by year so that two A courses have been given since the end of 1966.

QC Circle organization

As shown in figure 1, the QCC is divided into four committees and each department has a QC organization under the direction of the main QC office for the whole company. The QC programme is arranged to fit the needs of each shop, while the basic essentials of the programme cover the entire company. In each section of the company there is a circle leader (section chief) who is in charge of the circle operations in that section. To promote the programme in the company as a whole, these leaders meet and give final approval to circle conferences and all other functions.

QC Circle operation

Except for general matters drawn up by the main QC office, annual programme plans and principles are determined individually by the department organizations. Under the sponsorship of the QCC and main QC office, all staff members, from group chiefs up, hold an 'Annual Programme Meeting.' This meeting is intended to clarify, for all employees, the circles' goals. In March, a meeting is

Figure 1 Circle organization

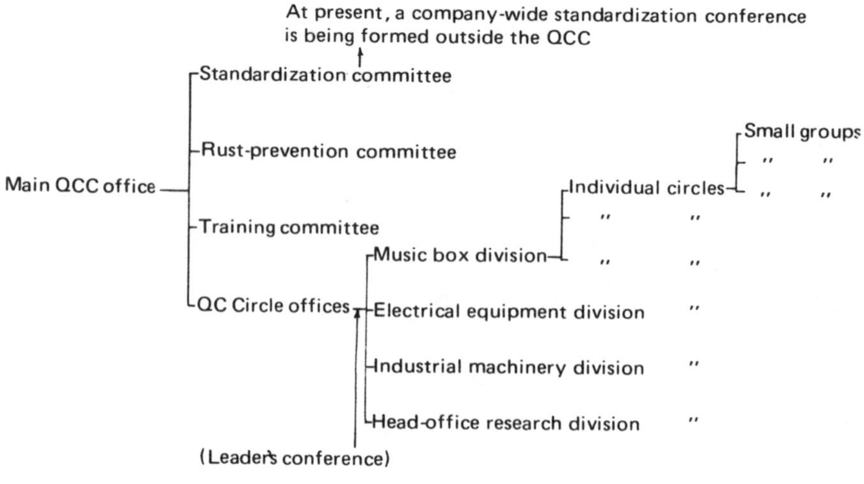

At present, a company-wide standardization conference is being formed outside the QCC

Main QCC office
— Standardization committee
— Rust-prevention committee
— Training committee
— QC Circle offices
  — Music box division
  — Electrical equipment division
  — Industrial machinery division
  — Head-office research division
— Individual circles
  — Small groups

(Leader's conference)

held by each of the QC organizations to present the progress report for the previous year. This also serves to acquaint the workers with circle programmes.

Employees holding QC qualifications are eligible to become circle leaders. Ninety-five per cent of the circle leaders are from the first-line supervisory staff in the group chief or skilled worker class. The office staff and QC Circle leaders work in close liaison. Recently, almost all the first-line supervisory staff have acquired the QC qualification and more women employees and those in the 'chief' class are obtaining it. These people have become active as

Table 4 Training system and range

Training system	Leader	Range	Contents and models
Sectional conference	Section chiefs	Skilled workers and other related staff	Highest intra-section meeting once or twice a month, check actual results, basic principles, basic training, circle operation, appraisals, discussions, decisions
Course conference	Section and subsection chiefs	Skilled workers circle, and group leaders	Subsection conferences once or twice a month, basic training, field trips, reports of exchanges
Case study meetings	Subsection and group chiefs circle and group leaders	Circle members	Recent case studies investigated by each circle, problem points, held when problem arises or weekly or monthly
QC line reports	Subsection and group chiefs circle and group leaders	Circle members	Case reports from each circle once every six months
IE study group	Full-time staff	Anyone interested	Voluntary study groups once a week, outside working hours
QC study group	Subsection and group chiefs, QC members, full time staff		Circle leader presides over discussion of shop needs
OJT	Group leaders	Circle members all employees, anyone interested	During and outside working hours
Printing of QC news	Manufacturing and technical department, subsection chiefs	All employees	Six times a year QC and ZD training organ

circle members or leaders of smaller groups within the circles. In 1968, there were 120 circles and 230 groups organized.

Leaders training and method of determining Circle goals

The leaders training system including follow-up courses for those with QC qualifications is organized basically as shown in table 4. Training is conducted either during or outside working hours, depending on shop requirements.

When the QC Circles were formed, voluntary management was emphasized and many goals were set at the workers' own initiative. However, at present, as shown in figure 2, basic goals are set for the factory as a whole including stipulations as to the environ-

Figure 2 Diagram showing organization of conference to check progress of basic control points.

Line		
Production sections	All production sub-chiefs, group chiefs, chief leaders Inspection section sub-chiefs, group chiefs, leader Executives	Conference to check the progress of the goals of each circle

Conference to check progress of basic control points

Staff	
Technical section	Those in charge of quality, production techniques, planning
Control section	Those in charge of planning and engineering
Control department improvement section	Those in charge of IE
Purchasing price	Those people in charge of purchasing

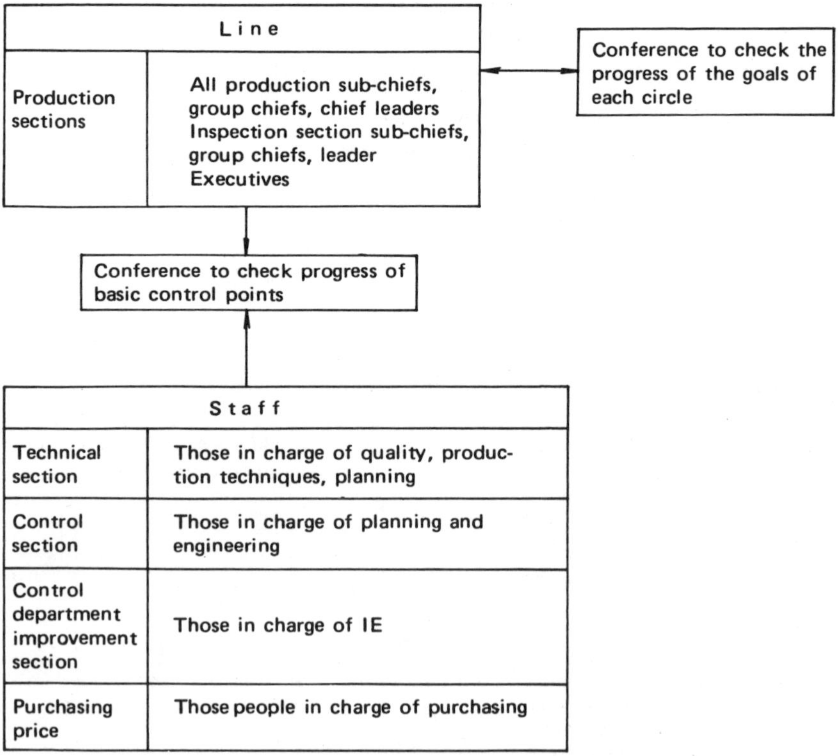

mental conditions which must be maintained by the individual employees during working hours.

The goals of the groups which make up the circles can generally be classified as follows: improving the quality of work, lowering work losses, increasing productivity, meeting daily schedules, and improving human relations and the shop environment, as well as safety conditions and other factors beneficial to the circle programme. All employees are responsible for improvement of the basic factors as shown in the outline of progress meeting reports (see table 5). Therefore, the leader of each circle is responsible for creating a balance between the prescribed goals and the voluntary goals of the workers as well as teaching the workers how to analyze problems.

Reporting results at conferences

Two meetings are held annually to report the progress of each circle. As can be seen in figure 3, the yearly number of cases has increased so much that the company-wide QC Circle conference is limited to representative circles from each department. In the second half of 1966, 260 case studies were reported. Generally, there are only two case report meetings a year, but case study and experience meetings are held whenever the circles feel that they are necessary. The reports are made up as follows:

Table 5 Contents of progress meeting reports

Section	Contents
Quality	Customer requirements, shipping inspection, individual processes, quality techniques of previous processes.
Production	Production output of each type of product, number shipped and number put into storage.
Efficiency	Objective specified time (O.S.T.).
Error losses	Defects in articles process by oneself, defects in articles processed by others; statistics, calculation of losses per unit.
Absenteeism	Details of reasons for absenteeism.
Non-productive	(Time not spent directly in production) Morning and evening assemblies, OJT, QC, ZD, etc.
Rationalization	Idea; execution; follow-up.
Subsidiary materials	Monthly expenditures, expenditures per unit.

AIM: Is the aim or purpose good or not; does it 'hit the mark'?
METHOD: Is the method used to the utmost or not?
RESULTS: Is it effective, how much money is spent, is it profitable?
EFFORTS: Are the circle members trying hard or not?
CIRCLE PROGRAMME: General condition of the circle programme, study groups, how the goals were determined, etc.
PRESENTATION: Is the presentation well done, is it easy to understand?

A panel of judges consisting mainly of group leaders evaluate the reports on the basis of these six points. The reports are ranked in order of merit, and monetary awards, plaques, or certificates are presented.

There are many arguments both for and against this method but in any case it has proven highly effective as an incentive for the circle members.

Evaluation and awards

It is a very difficult matter to evaluate the achievements of the circle movement. Any form of judgement comes up against the problem of working toward new goals. This is an indispensable condition to be fulfilled if the programme is to continue over a long period.

The award system is outlined in figure 4. The awards are planned according to the needs of the individuals in conjunction with the introduction of the ZD movement. The awards are in the form of money and certificates as well as memorial badges and photographs related to ZD and QC.

The awards are always based on actual results with considerations given to voluntary goals. Awards are determined on the basis of individual reports and discussions among the leaders.

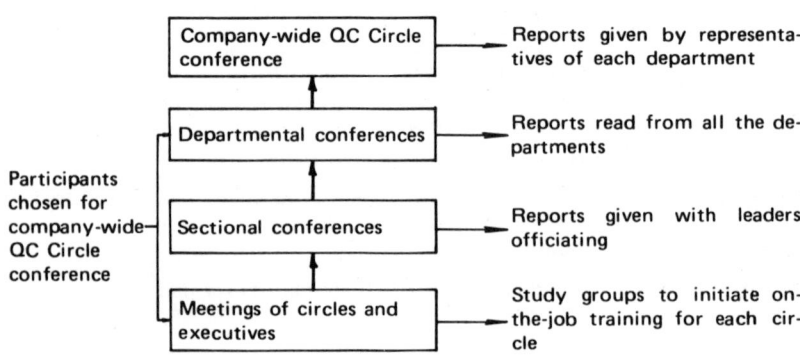

Figure 3 QC conference (to report results).

QC CIRCLE MOVEMENT APPLIED TO SHOP REQUIREMENTS

The QC Circle programme and training procedure for Sankyo Seiki has been described above. In this company, all the production departments except the optical department are located in the same

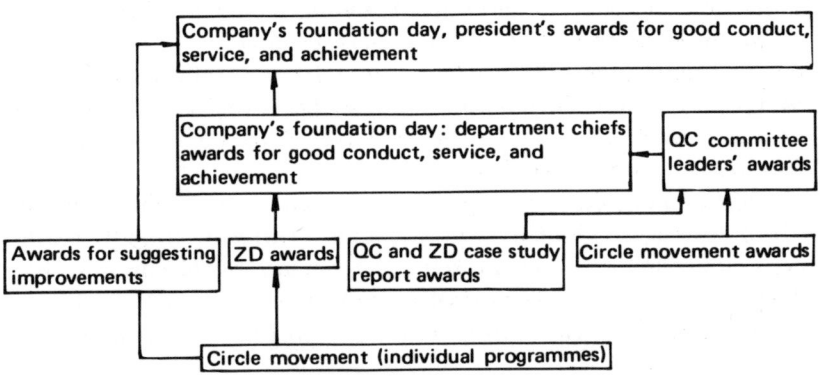

Figure 4 Award system

Figure 5 Individual goal system

E line { ZD group / QC circle — Establishing goals: work planning sheets		Section chiefs	Sub—section chiefs	Circle leaders	Chief group leaders
(Circle the appropriate choice) Subject: 1. Improving efficiency, reducing number of steps 2. Improving quality 3. Cost reduction, defect reduction 4. Improvement of working conditions 5. Improving human relations 6. Self-study		Establishment date: Revision date:		Process name	
				Group name	
				Employee's name	
This month's items (as definite and numerically detailed as possible) 1) 2)		Conformation, self-evaluation			
Item No.	Name of item	10 5	20 15	30 25	Progress memo
1					
2					

197

place but the type of goods they produce and various matters relating to the goods produced are completely different so that QC or ZD movements must be adopted according to the particular needs of each shop. One of the main reasons that the QC Circle movement has developed so rapidly in the last two or three years is that workers with the QC qualification have become circle leaders and are also the most active among members of the circles.

The importance of training has again been confirmed. However, it is extremely difficult to achieve success with training alone: In the QC Circle movement, training must be closely connected with the daily work in order to be effective. This became especially clear in the case of Sankyo Seiki.

When looking back, the QC movement has been highly effective in promoting the QC Circle programme. Previously the QC movement depended entirely on self-development, but from now on, attempts are being made to shift towards control of goals. This can be seen from the form shown in figure 5, entitled 'Individual Goal System.'

All circle members can understand the goal system and every month some goal is set which they can apply to their work. With this system, the worker can endeavour to improve his own work. This system was put into practice at the end of 1966 and is already proving to be highly effective. However, this does not mean that the QC Circle movement must follow the above pattern. The movement must be in accordance with the requirements of the individual shops. Future problems will no doubt arise concerning the means by which advisors formulate group goals and analyze operation principles.

Case 18

Elimination of inspection in the 'A' packing process

Mamoru Tanaka, et al.[*]

The Koganei Manufacturing Co. has two plants. The main plant in Koganei City, Tokyo, produces air valves, cutting tools, and precision finishing equipment. The Komagane plant produces automatic centralized lubrication equipment for use in large vehicles (buses, trucks, etc.) and industrial machinery. This is a medium sized company with a total of 500 employees.

Introduction and progress of the QC movement

QC was introduced in this plant when it was built, in 1961. Prior to this, QC activities were carried out in the main plant by the Quality Control Section. When the Komagane plant was constructed, the Quality Control Section in the main plant provided much helpful advice and information.

At that time, QC consisted of a random acceptance inspection and the preparation of a control chart for processing. QC was mainly in the hands of the foremen. However, QC based so much on mathematics has its limitations and therefore QC Circles were formed to develop techniques which were easy to understand and could be implemented freely by the workers. Circle members have since gone on to read reports at prefectural conferences, foremen's meetings, and QC Circle conferences as well as participate in tours of other plants.

---

[*] Mamoru Tanaka, Toshio Kobayashi, Takuro Kitahara, Noboru Ikeda, and Fujio Hayashi are all QC Circle members, at the Komagane Factory, Koganei Manufacturing Co.

As this movement has progressed, considerable stress has been placed on the assumption that the workers should be responsible for the products they produce and therefore we have tried to develop a situation in which the worker always checks whether his work is good.

Precautions for all processes were taken from the company's industrial standards by the plant advisors and compiled for all of the processes. Once the circles were formed, these precautions were thoroughly checked and confirmed by all employees during the manufacturing process.

One of the things that all circle members noted as these activities progressed was to make good products they required good parts. Workers outside the circle were trained by partially utilizing the QC Circles to promote the development of voluntary inspections. This has shown itself to be highly effective.

Below are described practical examples concerning these activities both inside and outside the company.

Case study: Elimination of inspection in the 'A' packing process (Manual pump circle)

Both manual and electric pumps are produced in the Komagane plant by 15 men and women. The QC Circle meets at least once every month and the group leader is selected by the circle members.

Reason for choosing the theme

November, 1967 was designated as QC Month and 'Let's eliminate errors due to carelessness' was chosen as the theme for the entire plant. Our group, however, decided to treat this problem in greater detail and selected the theme 'Completely eliminate defects from the packing process and thus do away with the need for any inspection' to be achieved within one year.

For technical reasons the packing process inspection is in the hands of inspectors who carry out all inspections on all products (parts inspections, external view, packing condition, etc.) Therefore, these inspectors require considerable time for their work and for that reason inspection should be eliminated as much as possible.

Basic plan and means of implementation

The following points were considered when establishing the steps to be taken to eliminate inspections.

ELIMINATION OF INSPECTION IN THE 'A' PACKING PROCESS

1 There are various causes of defects but in most cases, they originate with the worker himself. Therefore, we decided to first eliminate the defects due to carelessness, leaving those due to other causes until later.
2 Essentially, the worker should to some extent judge whether the products which he has made are good or not. The worker should be responsible for what he has produced.

Our circle then took the following steps:
1 The items and specifications concerning individual checks of workmanship were clearly defined and a thorough self-check was devised.
2 When there was a problem concerning the quality or installation of previously processed parts, these parts must always be checked in the subsequent processing step so that the manufacturing specifications and employee's checklist will be closely followed.
3 When the daily processing schedule is difficult to maintain, normal processing will be disrupted and the probability of defects will increase. To prevent such cases, the advisors discussed the matter sufficiently beforehand with the persons in charge so that the proposed schedules were not unreasonable.

Progress

As was mentioned above, the QC circle met once a month after the QC Month in 1967. At these meetings, countermeasures were prepared and put into effect using Pareto diagrams drawn from checklists compiled by the inspectors of inspection conditions. The QC Circles in charge of these inspections held a joint meeting and exchanged various opinions and aired problems concerning these inspections. They also endeavored to show clearly recent trends and specifications which have been adopted.

From January, 1968, the number of defects in electric pumps has decreased markedly, and in June only one pump had a defect due to adhesion of dirt.

In July another combined inspection circle meeting was held and from the actual results so far, it was decided to switch from total inspections back to random inspections. All employees decided to try to completely eliminate all inspections from October, but before that time it became possible to eliminate one machine.

Only the progress of one part of this movement has been outlined above. Circle members work together at lunch time and before work starts in the morning, which is enhancing the effectiveness of the circle (see figure 1).

Effectiveness

As mentioned above the greatest effectiveness was achieved through the cooperation of the circle members. Up to the present, results are as follows.
1. By the elimination of one machine, time was reduced by 20 hours per month.
2. Individual responsibility is now much more clearly accepted than before.
3. By exchanging opinions on several occasions with other departments (especially the inspection department), mutual cooperation has been instituted in fields other than quality control.

In order to increase the present high level of quality control, the problem of training new employees will arise. All members of the circle feel that QC training must be given to new workers together with their initial job training.

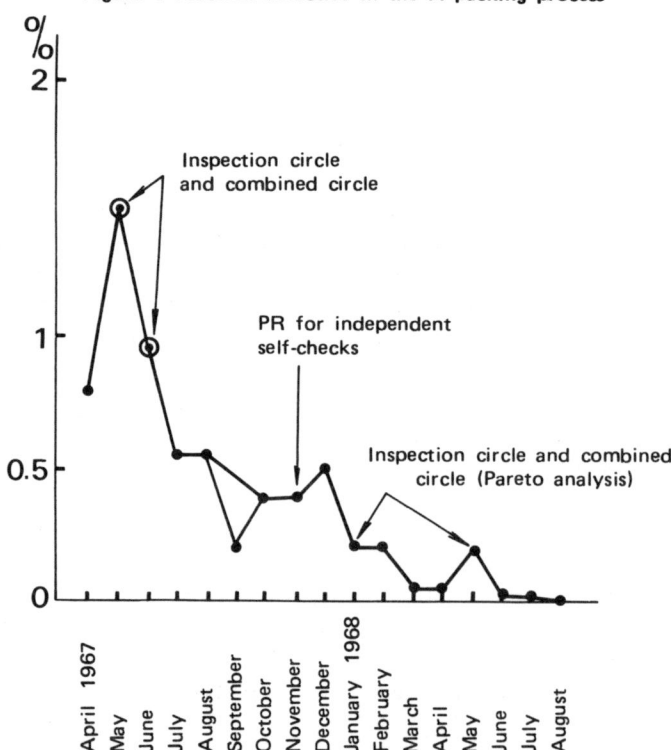

Figure 1 Fraction defective in the A packing process

Case study: Elimination of inspection in the 'B' packing process (GK Circle)

Our shop produces distribution valves and distribution selector valves for lubrication equipment by means of an assembly-line system. There are three QC Circles which are limited both in time and in spirit because of the conditions imposed by the assembly line. They are however doing their utmost to improve the manufacturing process, and promote quality control. Activities of one of these circles, the GK circle, is introduced here.

Theme and plans

The original circle was made up mostly of women, for which reason there was little serious discussion at circle meetings. To improve this situation, the circle was divided into three in 1966. In November, 1967, the same theme was chosen as in the electric pump shop, 'elimination of inspection in the packing process.' It was decided that the goal would be switch from total inspection to random inspection by October and the QC group made 'establishment of quality during processing' its basic idea. The aim was to reduce major defects which amounted to as much as 0.7 per cent, to less than 0.3.

Progress

First, the following steps were taken.
1 Items for individual checking by the workers themselves were compiled and explained for each process step.
2 The attitude that even small errors undetected in previous steps should be detected was fostered.
3 All workers were given as many chances as possible to discuss matters and learn together so as to see the significance of their own work.

The QC Circles have begun to teach the workers what the significance of their work is in the over-all process. Some rotation of workers for 'A', 'B', and 'C' processes is being done so that they may learn to go on to train the workers during their own work and before the inspection, to detect errors made during previous processes.

To produce good products, workers must know the purpose, content, and significance of their work. For example, even if the worker only drills a single hole, he should know at least the basic reason for the hole as well as the general application of the pro-

mutual understanding of the various process steps and this is proving to be highly effective.

These steps are being repeated again and again whenever possible. At the monthly QC Circle meeting, circle members confirm these principles by means of Pareto diagrams and carefully examining their own work so as to be able to devise and carry out improvements.

As a result of these efforts, the fraction defective decreased from April and the goal of 0.3 per cent defects has been lowered to 0.02 to 0.03 per cent (see figure 2).

Effectiveness

The effectiveness of the programme was shown in the following ways.

1 The fraction defective decreased steadily toward the set goal and even dropped below the goal so that random inspection was possible from October.

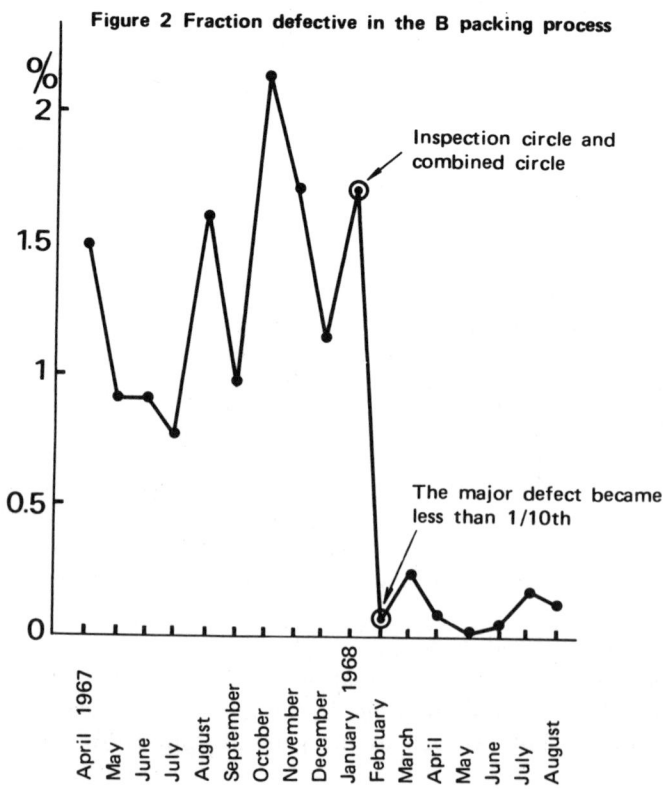

Figure 2 Fraction defective in the B packing process

2 The workers' knowledge of the significance of their own work has increased.
3 There is no problem concerning the responsibility for inspection by sections dealing with only one part of the product.

The per cent defective is extremely low but there are some instances of interference in functioning due to the presence of defects and it is essential to make the process steps even more stabilized.

The achieve higher goals and reach the stage where no inspection is necessary, QC Circles face the difficult problem of relying on the assistance and cooperation of related departments. Therefore, we must all endeavor to solve complex problems which must be eliminated before more improvements can be made.

Case study: Establishing quality standards for subcontractors' parts (Inspection Circle)

This programme resulted from a problem proposed by two sections and is being handled mainly by the inspection circle and those in charge of materials. Those in charge of QC are also rendering indirect assistance.

Reason for selecting the subject

Previously when the Komagane plant received parts from other plants, defects were common and this gave rise to delays and created confusion.

Even if the delivered parts were accepted, defects were bound to exist because only a sampling inspection was employed. If the tests were made stricter, the number of test samples increased and more steps were required. Too many parts accumulated for acceptance inspection and circulation was disrupted.

Therefore in accordance with the basic assumption of the QC group that good products need good parts, the pertinent work of the subcontractors was considered as part of the process of our company and therefore it was necessary to establish the habit of individual self-checks in the associated companies before they sent their parts to our company.

In this way, delays in parts delivery were eliminated and the number of defects in the work of the subcontractor decreased to the profit of both companies. Once the self-check system was established the lot rejection fell to the goal of less than one per cent. (This goal of less than one per cent had been established in July, 1967.)

Because subcontractors were involved, many difficult problems were present but the programme was able to proceed due to the patient cooperation of related departments.

Basic consideration and procedures

The first matter was to publicize the aims of the QC Circle and initiate training in the associated company so that they would always supply products of high quality. However, in order to insure quality would be high, the subcontractor had to increase the number of process steps and therefore might have sought an increase in the delivery price on the assumption that 'high quality means a high price.' However, strong warnings were given that the unit price must not be increased because QC is not an excuse for making profits.

The delivered parts undergo inspection in our company to check whether the quality is being maintained by the subcontractor.

Second, if the quality of the delivered parts is stabilized and the lot rejection decreased, the acceptance inspection in our company can be simplified.

Third, it is planned that if this programme continues, the stage will be approached where inspections are completely unnecessary.

If the subcontractor supplies only products which have been closely checked, they can easily pass our acceptance tests.

Progress

The subcontractors are spread over a wide area, mainly in the Ina and Tokyo districts. It was decided to carry out this programme first in the Ina region, and then in Tokyo, because Ina is near the Komagane plant.

First, the aims of the programme were clearly explained to responsible people in the subcontracting companies. In order to avoid misunderstandings, these meetings were attended by all staff levels. For training and publicity purposes, the monthly QC newsletter was distributed in the subcontractor companies. Publicity was also given to the delivery conditions of other companies.

The effects of the programme were immediate in some companies and only gradual in others, but actual results began to appear in and after December 1968. Naturally, the per cent defective decreased. When the results became evident in a company, and the company was commended, the attitude arose that 'we cannot let that company get the better of us' and if the quality was low enough to result in rejection of a lot, it would be reported beforehand. Also, subcontractors' personnel met with our inspection people to confirm the quality of the parts.

When a supplier's products received a commendation, the company was presented with inscribed calipers or some similar measuring instrument which could be put to actual use in the factory. The reason for this was that if the workers were aware that they were using tools from a company which had commended their work they would try to use the awarded instruments to make sure that the dimensions, etc. were always exact, in order to maintain a high level of quality.

The results of this programme are shown in figure 3.

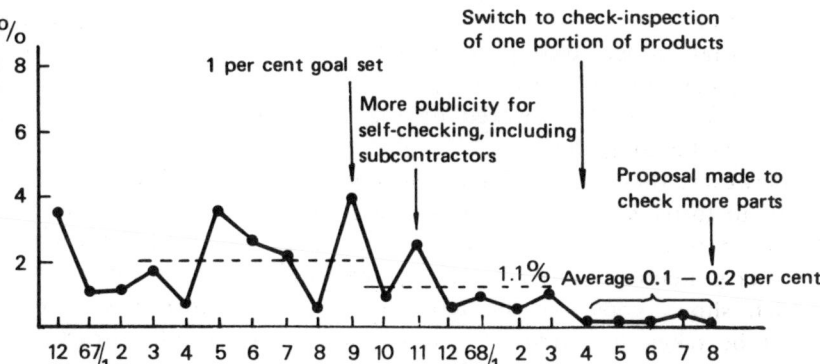

Figure 3   Defects in products from subcontractors in the Ina District

In all suppliers the tendency to employ self-checks became stronger in December 1967, and this became even clearer as the publicity drive came to an end. From April 1968, their parts became so good that it was possible to switch to a check inspection (from January 1967 to March 1968 not a single lot was rejected and there was no claim against any products from the users).

In September, 1968 the parts which were accepted only on the basis of a check inspection increased considerably and two or three of the subcontractors improved and stabilized the quality of their parts to such an extent that check inspections proved sufficient in all cases.

This programme was instituted in the Tokyo area around October 1968 and favourable results were soon evident.

Effectiveness

The effectiveness of the programme is evident from the following points.

1. The fraction defective in almost all companies dropped by 0.1 to 0.2 per cent and within one year there were almost no defects. (For most suppliers, defects were eliminated after a half year except for test products.)
2. The employees in our company have come to trust the suppliers more than before.
3. The number of inspections and the number of goods returned has decreased.
4. The time lost due to lot rejection is rapidly decreasing.
5. Technical improvements are becoming evident.

In the subcontractors, the effects are as follows:

1. The workers are taking a greater responsibility in regard to quality.
2. Mutual understanding with the receiver company (i.e. the Koganei Manufacturing Co.) is good.
3. Defects can be discovered during the processing, before they leave the company.

However, there are still some subcontractors who think it sufficient to think of quality assurance only at the final stage of their work; it is necessary that such subcontractors are provided with further guidance. There are also some who think that a company which shows good results need not conduct inspections. Care must be taken to narrow the differences between subcontractors.

Every year in the past, the plant managers announced their policy which, although differing in manner of expression, have in all instances strongly emphasized the need for striving to improve quality. The integrated efforts mainly of responsible people within the QC Circles have been effective in furthering this policy.

All QC Circles are striving to improve the teamwork which has been the basis for their success and it is hoped that they will become even more effective in the future.

The programmse and experiences of our company as described above is certainly not of any major importance in itself but the fact that everyone makes an effort and attains greater self-confidence is an important achievement.

It cannot be said that the site of the factory is ideal geographically but this negative factor has been compensated for by the efforts of employees.